CALLED TO ATTRACTION

CASCADE COMPANIONS

The Christian theological tradition provides an embarrassment of riches: from Scripture to modern scholarship, we are blessed with a vast and complex theological inheritance. And yet this feast of traditional riches is too frequently inaccessible to the general reader.

The Cascade Companions series addresses the challenge by publishing books that combine academic rigor with broad appeal and readability. They aim to introduce nonspecialist readers to that vital storehouse of authors, documents, themes, histories, arguments, and movements that comprise this heritage with brief yet compelling volumes.

TITLES IN THIS SERIES:

CALLED TO ATTRACTION

*An Introduction to
the Theology of Beauty*

BRENDAN THOMAS SAMMON

 CASCADE *Books* · Eugene, Oregon

CALLED TO ATTRACTION
An Introduction to the Theology of Beauty

Cascade Companions 38

Cascade Books
An Imprint of Wipf and Stock Publishers
199 W. 8th Ave., Suite 3
Eugene, OR 97401

www.wipfandstock.com

PAPERBACK ISBN: 978-1-62032-469-1
HARDCOVER ISBN: 978-1-4982-8791-3
EBOOK ISBN: 978-1-5326-1418-7

Cataloging-in-Publication data:

Names: Sammon, Brendan Thomas, author.

Title: Called to attraction : an introduction to the theology of beauty / by Brendan Thomas Sammon.

Description: Eugene, OR : Cascade Books, 2017 | Series: Cascade Companions 38 | Includes bibliographical references.

Identifiers: ISBN 978-1-62032-469-1 (paperback) | ISBN 978-1-4982-8791-3 (hardcover) | ISBN 978-1-5326-1418-7 (ebook)

Subjects: LCSH: God—Beauty. | God—Name. | Aesthetics—Religious aspects—Christianity.

Classification: BR115.A8 S36 2017 (print) | BR115.A8 S36 (ebook)

Manufactured in the U.S.A.   10/24/17

For Jim Skerl,
in whom I first saw the Beauty
of a Living Theology

CONTENTS

ACKNOWLEDGMENTS

THE COMPLETION OF THIS project would not have been possible without the help and support of a number of people. To each of them I owe a debt of gratitude that I hope this small work in some way begins to repay. This project was first conceived in conversations with Chad Pecknold, whose encouragement and friendship have been invaluable in too many ways to enumerate. My gratitude is also owed to those friends and colleagues who either read chapters for me, or conversed with me about the book's contents: Daniel Wade McClain, Kevin Hughes, Matthew Boulter, Graham MacAleer, Trent Pomplun, Fritz Bauerschmidt, Gerard Jacobitz, Bill Madges, Allen Kierkeslager, Phil Cunningham, Bruce Wells, Jim Caccamo, Paul Aspan, Katie Oxx, Shawn Krahmer, Isra Yazicioglu, Adam Greggerman, David Carpenter, and Millie Feske. I would also like to thank Saint Joseph's University, whose generous summer research grant provided me with the financial means to work on a large portion of this book. As always, my deepest appreciation goes to my family, as well as *la mia famiglia Italiana*. My most sincere appreciation also belongs to those at my own Alma Mater in whom I first learned the beauty of theological thought and with whom I had the honor of teaching later in life, the faculty at St. Ignatius High School: Jim Brennan, Tom Healey, Paul Prokop, Gayle Scarivelli, James Hogan, Michael McLaughlin, Martin Dybicz, Daniel Galla, Michael Pennock, Lawrence Ober, SJ, and Timothy Kesicki, SJ. Thanks must also be given to the fine folks at Wipf & Stock, especially Christian Amondson and Charlie Collier, for their enduring patience during the process of completing this manuscript. This book is dedicated to the memory of James Skerl, in whom I first saw the beauty of a living theology; I could write a thousand books and it still would not repay the debt I owe to him and all of my first teachers. Above all, my gratitude goes to my wife Chiara, for all she does to afford me a life where I can study and teach this most blessed of subject matter, and to my two children Liam and Raffaele who encouraged me in a number of important ways. Anything that is edifying in this book is a result of the graces given through all of these, while anything in error is my own.

Brendan Thomas Sammon
Feast of All Souls' Day, 2016

INTRODUCTION

EVERYONE KNOWS WHEN HE or she is touched by something beautiful. Beauty is such that it does not require an advanced degree, an insider's knowledge, or any studious labor to be recognized. It appears when and where it wants to, and the human person cannot but submit to its appearance. This is not to say that when it appears to one person, others must also see it in that moment the way that person sees it. Rather, beauty's immense power to take hold of a person derives from the fact that its reach extends to the radical particularity of the person where it inhabits his or her subjective experience. Yet like the enthusiastic friend who refuses to let another stay home from the celebration, beauty's indwelling stirs us to a place of glorious unrest, provoking us out of ourselves into its shared splendor. Its universal power is also its capacity to inhabit the particular, while its power to inhabit the particular is also a power that steals us from ourselves, carrying us off into an unimaginable glory.

This is not to deny the riches that one may receive from inquiring more closely into the nature of beauty and the traditions that have contemplated it in various ways.

In fact, beauty is such that it also provokes a deep sense of wonder, inspiring thought to explore its ever-mysterious content in a variety of ways: philosophically, theologically, artistically, culturally, socially, etc.

Arising within this wonder a number of questions may be provoked and in large measure this book is a result of such provocation. Some of the more significant questions at the foundation of this book are: what if beauty's immense power to reach deep into the subjective particularity of a person and take hold of that person is invested with divine intentionality? What if beauty is the form that the divine desire takes in the world of shared experience? Or even more, what if beauty is the very presence of God in a world desperately trying to find Him?

The answers to conditional questions such as these are complex, and it is hoped that what follows might in some way begin to throw light on this complexity. It is the purpose of this book to offer a brief introduction into what could be called a theology of beauty, or what is more commonly called today theological aesthetics. If this book employs the language of the *theology of beauty* rather than *theological aesthetics* it is not because it rejects the latter, but rather because of the principles at the heart of the present work.

The first and most foundational principle at the heart of our examination is a principle that has long informed and given formation to the developing Christian theological tradition but that in large measure has been forgotten. It is a principle that from the beginning had been gestating in the womb of the Western intellectual tradition but that only came to full term sometime around the fifth century. This principle, quite simply stated, is that *beauty is a divine name*, one of the names of God.

Naturally, the idea of a divine name provokes some other important questions: What is a divine name? What could it possibly mean to name God? What theological advantage is there is looking to the tradition of the divine names? Why is it important to examine the phenomenon of beauty from the perspective that sees it as a divine name? Again, all of these questions will be explored in the pages that follow, but a few of the notable points are worth foregrounding here.

A DIVINE NAME APPROACH

First, as it is understood according to the tradition that bears its name, a divine name is an outward flow of God's very self that comes to inhabit certain formal qualities in the world. Alongside beauty some of these more well-known names include goodness, truth, love, being, and wisdom. As qualities of almost all commonly shared human experiences, these divine names could be called God's public identity, or the appearance that God takes in the world outside of those faith traditions that have arisen around what is believed to be God's revealed identity. In this sense, what is "public" stands in contrast, not to what is "private," but rather what is "endemic," "intimate," or what is "internal to a community." That is to say, where God's revealed identity gives rise to an endemic and intimate relationship constituted by specific forms of faith, dogma, liturgical and sacramental rites, the divine names as God's public self-presentation give rise to more general, socio-cultural forms of these. For this reason, the divine names tradition provides an invaluable resource of all theological discourses.

Second, it is within the divine name tradition where not only is beauty first identified with God's very self, but also where beauty first becomes a phenomenon of explicit theological inquiry. The ancient world had flirted with the idea that beauty is something in itself holy, sacred, and for that perhaps even divine. But it is not until the belief that God assumes a human nature, that is to say it is not until the doctrine of the Incarnation, that the identity between God and beauty becomes an established fact. For prior to this event, beauty proved to be ambiguous to thought, inhabiting both the material world of sensible things as well as the immaterial world of spiritual things. How could these two worlds be brought together without compromising one for the other? For the thinkers of the Christian theological tradition, the person of Jesus Christ provided the answer because in him there was, for the first time ever, a perfect comingling of divine and human, Creator and creature, spirit and matter, and it was a comingling that at once preserved the integrity of each precisely by bringing them into perfect unity.

BEAUTY OR THE AESTHETIC?

Within contemporary thought, there is something of a tension between beauty and what is today commonly referred to as aesthetics. Within the last couple of centuries, a notable shift has occurred that has replaced beauty with the aesthetic. This shift involved a movement away from beauty that was thought to be "out there" in the world independent of human cognition into aesthetic perception thought to be "in here," that is, within the experience of human consciousness.

In light of this shift, it becomes necessary to explain why the language of the present work continues to speak of a theology of beauty more than a theological aesthetic. To be sure, it is not the contention of this book that the two are at odds but rather that they have an organic continuity.

When appropriate, we will speak of a theological aesthetic but always as one contemporary form of a theology of beauty. All theological aesthetics in some way involves the phenomenon of beauty even if only as an historical necessity. Even if the aesthetic has replaced beauty, it has done so only by virtue of its historical emergence *from* beauty. The reasons for speaking of a theology of beauty rather than a theological aesthetic are in many ways tied to this relationship, and can be enumerated more specifically as follows.

First, beauty is more original and therefore more historically rooted than the aesthetic. As this is an introduction to the relationship between theology and beauty, it bears as much an historical dimension as a systematic one. Therefore, for the sake of historical accuracy and to avoid foisting upon the past an "aesthetic" sense that was never there, ours will be primarily a theology of beauty, that is to say, an inquiry into the nature and role of beauty within the theological project.

Second, there is a practical advantage for using the language of beauty rather than aesthetics. For one thing, because it is more common, the word beauty has a greater degree of relate-ability than the aesthetic. That is to say, most people today have a better common grasp of beauty than they do aesthetics. As we will see, the whole notion of the aesthetic as it used today, despite having roots in the ancient Greek tradition, derive primarily from the eighteenth century. This makes the many ways in which the term "aesthetics" is used today sometimes confused and confusing, suggesting the need to invoke something more reliable than the aesthetic. For another thing, beauty can inhabit just about any world it confronts, whether it is the world of science, history, economics, politics, philosophy or theology. It is unclear whether the same can be said for the aesthetic. Ever since it became configured as a separate science of its own in the eighteenth century, the aesthetic has sought to carve out a domain to identify its unique corresponding purview. And although this may have had the effect of elevating the significance of aesthetic phenomena, it also separated them from other discourses. Beauty is not limited in this same sense and is therefore freer than the aesthetic, capable of being found in every discourse.

Third, using the language of beauty rather than the aesthetic ensures that our inquiry begins in the world of things, the world outside the human mind. This is not to reject the importance of subjective experience and consciousness, what might be called the world inside the mind; quite to the contrary, one of beauty's most powerful features concerns its impact upon these internal dimensions of human experience. Rather, focusing on beauty and thus something outside the human mind not only enables a greater degree of harmony with the tradition to be explored, but also provides a communal orientation to the variety of subjective experiences. Beauty's power is perhaps experienced most intensely in the way it pulls a person out of him or herself toward something that was previously beyond the person's individual consciousness. The language of beauty will facilitate a deeper awareness of this.

INTRODUCTORY SCOPE

As the title states, this book is an introduction into what is otherwise a much more complicated and diverse field of theological discourse. Not everybody will be satisfied, therefore, with the choices made within these pages to foreground certain dimensions while either backgrounding or leaving out other dimensions. As an introduction, however, it is hoped that what is foregrounded inspires a desire for further inquiry. The content of what follows does not intend to present a complete picture of the theological tradition of beauty. Rather, the intention of the content with the pages that follow is twofold.

The first intention is to provide a "forest" view of the theological tradition of beauty by examining some of the more prominent "trees," so to speak. The selection of the theological figures and ideas, what constitutes the "trees," derives not only from a sense of the author's own personal interest, but also from the contribution that these figures and ideas make to the vision of a theology of beauty being presented.

The second intention follows from the particularity of this vision: to recognize that beauty is not only a phenomenon that attracts intellectual inquiry, but also enters into that very inquiry, providing thought, or reason, with significant resources for its various operations. This is a vision of beauty that follows from the association of beauty with Christ; like the study of Christ, the study of beauty is simply less effective if it is done from some neutral, disinterested position. Rather, to truly understand the phenomenon of beauty one must enter into it and allow it to enter into one's own habits of mind. The second intention of this book, then, is to examine the ways in which this might happen. It does this not only by examining beauty from the perspective in question, but also by looking at some of the most significant historical examples of beauty's intimacy with reason.

Above all, this book is an introduction that serves as a general guide to the relationship between beauty and God in the Christian theological tradition. As a guide, it is hoped that this book may inspire a more careful and diligent study of this relationship by provoking a desire to discover not only the depths to which the ideas within these pages open, but also to discover the ways in which other figures in the Christian tradition and beyond sought the divine beauty.

Most importantly, it is hoped that this book inspires in the reader at least a modicum of desire to seek the divine beauty in all things.

1

ANCIENT ORIGINS OF BEAUTY'S ASSOCIATION WITH GOD

TODAY, WE TEND TO believe that beauty is in the eye of the beholder. But has it always been this way? For the ancient world, beauty was not in the eye of the beholder, or at least not *only* in the eye of the beholder. In part, this was due to the fact that the "beholder" as we understand her today had not yet been thrust into the cosmic spotlight, had not yet become the center of the universe's orbit. Rather the cosmos itself held center stage, mystifying its inhabitants with an allure that transcended all manners of finite knowing and intellectual effort.

The sheer fact of existence—that there is anything at all rather than nothing—was at one time so captivating that it inspired human beings to unparalleled degrees of wonder and awe. Human beings found themselves immersed in and part of a cosmic order that was somehow both present to *and* far beyond the human capacity to know it, think it, and understand it. In its presence, the cosmos invited the human intellect to engage its many material and immaterial forms. In its being beyond, however, the cosmos maintained a distance through which echoed its call to the human intellect to ever-higher phenomena, ideas, and mysteries. This call, this reverberating echo of the cosmos, resonating in both present things and from beyond, was where beauty revealed itself for the first time.

This chapter explores the way in which this call first echoed throughout the ancient world. Although almost every ancient civilization responded with comparable vigor to this call, two stand out for how they influenced the Christian theological tradition, namely, the Jews and the Greeks. The Jews heard this call issue from the God who creates the world, who calls forth a chosen people, and who establishes a covenant with his chosen people. The Greeks heard this call as the attraction of the cosmos itself, both in its material and immaterial forms, both in its immanence and in its transcendence. As this chapter will show, each of these calls embodied the origins of how beauty not only first manifested itself among worldly phenomena, but also revealed its association with the divine.

BEAUTY IN ANCIENT ISRAEL

For the ancient Jews, God's cosmic call issued from beyond them while simultaneously reverberating from within them. It is important to stress that this call was not seen as something to be analyzed or subjected to philosophical inquiry. Rather it was a call that summoned a people and cultivated a response. Like a soothing melody resonating across a barren wilderness, God's call to Israel was understood as salvific, recreating them as a people in the call itself. As the psalmist expresses this: "God drew me from the desolate pit, out of the miry bog, and set my feet upon a rock, making my steps secure. He put a new song in my mouth, a song of praise to our God" (Ps 40:2–3). God's call was conceived as a new song put into the mouth of Israel, a song that in its newness formed them and aroused them to respond with singing.

There are many forms that this ancient Hebraic singing assumed, though the Hebrew Scriptures are perhaps the most significant. These sacred texts are the result of a relationship between the emerging Jewish community and the God through whom, in whom, and with whom they sing. They also provide the foundation for the origins of how God came to be identified as beauty.

Genesis

The Jewish account of the beginning of God's call can be traced back to the creation narrative that begins in Genesis but continues to resonate throughout the Hebrew Scriptures as that call gathers a people to be God's dwelling place on earth. In the very first chapter of Genesis, God's call assumes linguistic form in the divine "let there be" (*yehiy 'or* in Hebrew, *fiat* in Latin, *genēthētō* in Greek). The author of Genesis has God utter this "let there be" as a way to call forth from the "formless void," that which is called forth on each of the six days of creation. It is a linguistic form that expressed the way in which God's call is itself constitutive of that which is called. In this sense, God's speaking is no mere shouting into the void but rather a creative force that makes something happen.

As presented by the text, this whole procedure, like the work of an artist, is a bringing forth of beauty. The author of Genesis uses the Hebrew word *tov* to describe God's own appraisal of what He Himself had brought forth after each day's work. If it seems odd to associate beauty with this process, it is because most translations render the word *tov* with the English "very good": "God looked at what he had brought forth and found it very good [*tov*]." However, as Hebrew scholars point out, the word *tov* has the sense of something well-made, which includes being attractive or pleasing when seen.[1] In the eyes of God, it might be said, what is good is also what is beautiful.

Creation is beautiful in this account because it is everywhere constituted by the order called forth by God himself. It is divine ordering that grants the gift of form to the unformed chaos. In giving form to what is without form, God opens the way by which creation may begin to conform to God's own being itself, may begin to fit with God. Only through this donation of form can things begin to appear in their specified distinctions as *this* tree, *this* mountain, *this* star, etc. And only when the primordial, unformed chaos becomes divinely in-formed in this way can it elicit the attraction that is associated with beauty. So here, in this earliest Hebraic text we find the first and most important attributes of beauty: order, proportion, harmony, or what could also be called fittingness.

Nowhere is this fittingness more evident than in the Garden. The dominant feature of this garden is its beauty, its attraction, its delight to look upon. The author of this second creation narrative, referred to as the Yahwist tradition, describes how "[o]ut of the ground the LORD God made to grow every tree that is pleasant to the sight and

1. See Brown, Driver, and Briggs, *A Hebrew and English Lexicon of the Old Testament*, 373b.

good for food" (Gen 2:9). For the Hebraic tradition, this passage could be considered the first distinction between the good and the beautiful, where the former appeals to the sense of taste (and smell by extension) and the latter appeals to the sense of sight. In the next chapter's temptation narrative this distinction appears again when referring to the forbidden tree, a tree harboring the knowledge of good and evil: ". . . the woman saw that the tree was good for food, and that it was a delight to the eyes. . ." (Gen 3:6). Here the good is associated with nourishment and taste, while beauty or delight is associated with seeing and being seen.

Everything in the garden is given to Adam and Eve that they might come to know their creator. And everything that adorns the garden is pleasing, delightful, and beautiful. Knowledge of God and of his creation, so the narrative seems to imply, is always and everywhere bound up with the beauty that draws desire ever higher. In this sense, then, beauty can be understood as the beginning of knowledge insofar as it constitutes the event that first provokes the intellect toward an object to be known. No knowledge can come about unless the known is first desired as something to be known, and beauty ensures such a condition. As the prohibited tree of knowledge of good and evil suggests, there is a risk—even a fatal danger—that comes when desire and knowledge are thus set free by beauty.

Exodus

In creating, it might be said, God reveals the way in which his creative power can give rise to an endless surplus of beings. And inasmuch as his creative power flows from the very substance of his being, it reveals that his being is an endless plenitude of formal content, or content out of which every form arises. God is capable of creating anything and everything. And since a thing is beautiful insofar as it has form—form identifies that aspect of a thing that enables it to be perceived, desired, and known—God's substance as an endless plenitude of formal content means that God is the most beautiful of all beauties; in fact, it can be said that when read in this way, the Genesis account of creation paints the picture of a God who is beauty itself.

This theory of beauty that derives from the Genesis narrative finds its complement in the narrative depicted in Exodus. It might be helpful to first recall the context. The Israelites, with whom God has chosen to establish a special covenant, have become slaves in Egypt. Year after year, decade after decade, the promise that God would send a deliverer remains unfulfilled. As Israel's cries to God grow louder, and their labor grows more difficult, a young Hebrew boy raised by Egyptian royalty grows into a virtuous Egyptian prince. When that young boy, Moses, comes to learn of his true origins, he takes upon himself the pain and suffering of his people and responds to God's call to lead them out of bondage. During the time of preparation, God tells Moses to go to the people of Israel and proclaim their captivity ended. Moses asks God to reveal His name in case the Israelites ask who this God is who has sent him. And it is here, in the revelation of God's name, that we find many important features of the nature of beauty and God's association with beauty, suggested in the Genesis account.

God reveals his identity to Moses in two interrelated ways. Both of these revelations indicate the way in which God identifies himself as a plenitude of formal content, that is, a limitless and unbounded source of all that is, was, and will be. First, God reveals himself with the name *Ehyeh asher Ehyeh*, most often translated by Christian scholars as "I am that I am" or "I am the one that is" (Exod 3:14). Many Jewish scholars, however, maintain that these translations fail to convey the sense of divine unboundedness that the Hebrew implies. A better translation, they explain, is "I will be what I will be" since this implies God's absolute and utter freedom to be—God can be whatever God wills to be.[2] God is the perfect "to be" because God's very being is the origin of all that was, is, and will be. God's being, it might be said, is a plenitude, or excess, of formal content, an endless reservoir of the power of existence whose gift of existence gives every being its form.

Second, the other name, the *HaShem*—also called the Tetragrammaton and represented with the letters YHWH— is used throughout Scripture as God's official use-name, appearing over 6,800 times. What is unique about this name is that it embodies a paradox insofar as it represents the verb "to be" in all three tenses simultaneously. It is a name that unites past, present, and future in one single utterance, signifying both eternality and mystery but also the concrete embodiment of being in and with the world. It also signifies the way in which God's official use-name captures the sense of the *Ehyeh asher Ehyeh* noted above, identifying God with a plenitude or surplus of form, an endless reservoir of the power of existing.

So what do these passages have to do with beauty? Most fundamentally they serve to confirm the idea, latent in the Genesis narrative, that all things that exist are endowed by God with beauty because God is beauty itself. To see this it is necessary to understand that the origins of beauty are deeply rooted in a theology of creation and revelation. Contrary to our late modern ways of thinking about beauty, the origins of beauty as testified to in Genesis and Exodus suggests a fuller, more complete, understanding of beauty that roots it in the very fabric of existence itself. A few suggestions offer themselves in light of this analysis.

2. Cf., e.g., Fields, *Torah Commentary for Our Times*, 19.

First and foremost, beauty identifies a principle of form: in the most primary way, beauty accounts for the particular form of any and every existing thing. That is to say, beauty is what makes a thing to be a particular, unique, thing that occupies this time and this space. A thing is beautiful because it has form, which enables it to be apprehended or perceived. And conversely, anything that is capable of being apprehended or perceived has form and is therefore *to some degree* beautiful.

Secondly, beauty identifies the root of attraction and interest. The word that scholars often use for something rooted in this way is "principle." Therefore, beauty can be identified as a principle of attraction or interest insofar as it is also the principle (or "root") of form. Only that which has form can ever attract the perception of another being, and as Genesis indicates, the divine giving of form makes things to be delightful to the eyes, or beautiful. Another way to describe this notion is to say beauty is that in a given thing, which allows it to attract the interest of another being. And in this way, beauty can also be identified as a principle of knowledge. All knowledge must begin with an initial moment of attraction of some kind, a moment where the desire to know it is provoked, and a thing's power to attract and provoke this desire derives from its beauty.

Above all, beauty is deeply and profoundly bound up with God's very being; simply put, God is beauty itself. More than a few passages in the Hebrew Scriptures bear witness to this.[3] In the Exodus narrative, the two names that God gives to Moses testify to the fact that God's very being, which ultimately no name can contain, is a plenitude or excess of formal content, an endless reservoir of the

3. E.g., Wis 5:16; 13:3, 5; Pss 8:5; 26:8; 29:2, 4; 48:2; 68:34; 71:8; 93:2; 96:6; 104:1; 145:5; 148:13; Sir 43:1, 9; Ezek 16:14; Job 37:22; 40:10; Isa 60:19.

power to exist. If beauty provides a thing its capacity to be what it is as an object that attracts others to itself, then God as the origin of all such things is supremely full of beauty, or supremely beautiful, or simply beauty itself. As such, it is God's very self that becomes the source of all attraction demonstrating how God's revelation of his identity also carries with it the idea that God's being, as beauty itself, is a power that calls all things to attraction. As bound up with God's identity, beauty is a gathering power that draws the diversity of particular, individual beings into a unity without in any way damaging either the diversity or the unity.

BEAUTY IN ANCIENT GREECE

At the same time that God was gathering a people to himself, elsewhere in the ancient world the Greeks were investigating, with unparalleled intellectual rigor, anything and everything that the world offered. The second century theologian Clement of Alexandria famously believed that "what God's Word was to the Jews, philosophy was to the Greeks." His point was not to place philosophy and divine revelation on the same level, but rather to extol the value of many achievements of Greek thought and to demonstrate its positive contribution to understanding the mystery of divine revelation. Nevertheless, Clement's insight also conveys two important truths.

First, God's speaking, intended for all human beings, takes different forms in different times and places. Although it could never finally take the place of divine revelation, Greek philosophy provided a valuable resource for comprehending its reception. Second, if, as the Genesis narrative implies, the whole of creation is itself one such form of divine communication, then it follows that examining the inner workings and hidden mysteries of the created order is not only helpful but essential for a complete reception of what God communicates. And even though the Greeks did not view the world as the creation of a single, all-loving, all-powerful God, they were deeply attracted to the natural world as if it were itself divine.

This is precisely where the Greek approach to beauty begins: in the cosmic call that echoes throughout the natural order. There were many Greek terms used to convey what today we simply refer to as "beauty" or "beautiful." Chief among them, however, was the word *kalos*, a derivative of the verb *kalō* meaning "to call." To the Greek mind immersed in philosophical thought, everything harbored the capacity to be an object of inquiry, to attract the intellect into knowledge of itself. And this meant that every single entity in the natural world was endowed with a power to call the mind to the knowable content that constituted that entity's unique being. This power to call, this *kalos*, as a universal power in all things, itself became an "object" of philosophical interest, furnishing the great thinkers of the Greek tradition with perhaps their loftiest, if not most difficult, object of inquiry.

Beauty was a philosophical theme treated by many of the Greek philosophers, and the literature produced during this period bears witness to the remarkable insights into beauty that characterize the Greek tradition. However, for the sake of brevity, the focus here will be on the two most influential Greek philosophers, Plato and Aristotle.

Plato

It is clear that for Plato, beauty is a phenomenon worthy of the most rigorous intellectual inquiry. It attracts, provokes, stirs emotions and affections, overwhelms, uplifts, energizes, yet stills both the mind and the heart. Beauty for Plato is like a relentless lover: it offers just enough of itself to entice one's passions, drawing the beloved in only to withdraw the moment it comes into view. Yet its withdrawal is less a waning and more of a deepening into itself; in its increasing self-offer the recipient is united more and more with beauty's mysterious content.

Beauty's mysterious nature is not a puzzle that Plato sought to solve. Unlike the Sophists with whom Plato's Socrates so often contended, Plato did not believe that human thought could rely on its own self-sufficiency. Rather, the power of human thought is found in something other that draws thought out of the comfort of the limits of its current domain. In other words, he was a thinker who was comfortable with the "unknown other" that is always at first a mystery. Perhaps the best evidence for this is found in his *Hippias Major*, a dialogue in which Socrates and Hippias undertake an inquiry into the nature of beauty asking whether it is possible to define beauty. After examining a few possible definitions (e.g., the profitable, the useful, the appropriate, the beneficial), Socrates, rejecting all these, declares his appreciation for that old proverb, "all that is beautiful is difficult."

The difficulty of beauty seems to derive from the fact that it attracts the desire for knowledge but refuses to fully conform to the common w ays by which we know. Beauty we might say explodes the limits of definition and discursive thought. At the same time, because it appears in real, concrete things, beauty continually and attractively offers itself as an object of inquiry, thus appealing to the discursive impulse within human knowledge and the need for definition.

How, then, can human thought engage such difficulty? Is there perhaps a power of the intellect whose capacity to penetrate phenomena like beauty is stronger than our normal modes of discursive reasoning? Is there a way of engaging the world that, without excluding certain common practices of knowing and thinking, transcends those practices in its capacity to both approach and receive what it desires? Plato's answer to this question, which in some ways parallels the Hebraic experience of intimacy with God, is a resounding "yes": there is a power available to the human person in her pursuit of loftier phenomena like beauty. That power, as Plato's celebrated *Symposium* clarifies, is love.

The origins of our experience of love, Socrates explains, are found in the beautiful things of the world that attract us to them. These beautiful things elicit our love by appearing beautiful to our senses. But as we grow, our love deepens by moving beyond the sensible aspects of their beauty to more spiritual aspects. For example, we are attracted to a person at first by the outward beauty he or she displays, but as our love grows we are drawn to a beauty that is unseen by the eyes and that resides in the soul of the person. Here, we become aware of the beauty of invisible things like ideas and thoughts. This in turn attracts us ever higher into the abundance of beauty at the source of all that is.

This beauty does not exist in any particular concrete forms, but is rather the absolute, simple, perfect and everlasting beauty that Socrates calls an "open sea of beauty." This beauty is beyond words, beyond knowledge, beyond anything that exists. It neither increases nor fades. It has no origin but is itself eternal. As such, it is the source of all beauty that we experience in the world. By moving from the beauty in material objects in the world to the beauty that is eternal and unchanging, Plato's account of beauty in the *Symposium* is significant for two primary reasons.

First, the ascent from the material to the spiritual is a power or energy that the Greeks called anagogy, from the verb *anagōgē* meaning "to ascend or uplift." It is a power that is closely associated with beauty since, as the Greeks believed, every encounter with beauty causes the percipient to be uplifted in some way. Beauty attracts a person to itself through a beautiful object. And persons are creatures motivated above all by love. "My weight is my love," Augustine would later write, "wherever I am carried my love is carrying me."[4] As we will see, Augustine's thought marks one of the earliest syntheses between the Biblical narrative of God's intimate love for creation and the Greek account of philosophical reflection. His ideas are everywhere pregnant with the anagogy that permeated the Greek consciousness. Love draws us into a beautiful thing, which then opens our desire to know the thing more intimately. In turn, further knowledge reveals deeper beauty, and the ascent continues.

Second, by referring all beauty in the world to the eternal, unchanging source of beauty, Plato marks a point at which Greek philosophy associates beauty with divinity. Plato did not go so far as to assert that God is beauty itself or that beauty is a god. However, in other dialogues like the *Phaedrus* and the *Timeaus* Plato seems to attribute a divine status to beauty so much so that this beauty bears characteristics similar to the God who reveals himself to Israel.

Nevertheless, important differences cannot be denied. For Plato beauty can only be considered divine insofar as it dwells in the eternal realm of Ideas. As an Idea, beauty is not a person or soul. It is rather an intelligible cause of beautiful things in the world. Still, since Plato believed that the Ideas were superior to the gods, his account established a firm foundation for beauty's divine status. In any case, what comes to light with Plato's understanding of beauty remains significant for the association of beauty with God that comes to mark the Christian tradition.

4. Augustine, *Confessions*, Bk. XIII.

Aristotle

Although Plato was Aristotle's teacher, Aristotle disagreed with some of Plato's most significant ideas. Aristotle's judgment over Plato's doctrine of beauty, however, is not so clear. There are passages where Aristotle maintains elements of Plato's view of beauty, such as beauty's transcendental status, viewing it as a reality independent of human experience or measure, and enduring beyond the transience of time.[5] But there is also evidence that suggests a gradual development within the timeline of Aristotle's writings away from Plato's more spiritual emphasis on beauty in favor of a more material configuration.

Aristotle also seemed at a loss on how to approach beauty in the context of his philosophy, which, less spiritually driven or idea-dependent than Plato's, rooted itself more completely in the world of things. In this respect, Aristotle confronted the same problems that had beset Plato when it came to beauty, only from the other side, as it were. For Plato, beauty's spiritual dimension was primary, which made it difficult to reconcile beauty's appearance in things of the world. For Aristotle, beauty's presence in things of the world is not an issue. Rather, beauty as something existing in itself and independent of things in the world becomes for Aristotle something suspect.

Nevertheless, Aristotle makes significant contributions toward understanding the nature of beauty and its association with the divine. Perhaps the most important is his conviction that beauty can be identified as *that which is desired for its own sake*.[6] To desire something for its own sake means to desire something, not for the end it might

5. *Metaphysics*, 1062b 15–1063a 5; *Nichomachean Ethics* 1123a 9–10 respectively.

6. Aristotle, *Rhetoric*, I, c. 9 (1366a 33).

bring about or the usefulness for acquiring something else, but simply for what it is in itself. This way of identifying beauty proves influential to the development of Western thought in general, and Christian thought in particular, for a number of reasons.

Above all, it distinguishes beauty from the good. It was a common belief among the Greeks that the good is that which all things desire. But as the good, it is desired as an end or as a means of acquiring some other end. Once the good is acquired it is no longer desired, although other, higher, goods may present themselves to desire thereafter. The question confronting the Greek mind was how is the desire for the good sustained if the good presents itself either as a not-yet-acquired end that is always beyond reach (and therefore desired) or as something already acquired and therefore no longer desired.

As Plato had already explained in the *Symposium*, even when something is desired as a not-yet-acquired end, the one who desires it must somehow have it in some way. Desire does not spontaneously generate itself in the one desiring the object desired. It is provoked by something other to it, drawn out of the desiring agent from something outside the agent itself. In this sense, when a good is desired it is somehow both present and absent simultaneously.

Aristotle was, of course, heir to the Greek tradition that conceived the good as that which all things desire, and consequently viewed the good as both the origin and end of existence. For Aristotle, however, origin and end are unified in desire. For in desiring a thing as a good, it is desired as an end. However, in being desired as an end, it is also the origin of that being's desire for it. Consider as an example the act of writing a book. If someone desires to write a book, the good—that is, the book itself—begins to come into being the moment that the desire for it as an end arises. So the good, in this Aristotelian dimension of the Greek tradition, is both an origin and end.

When Aristotle distinguished beauty as that which is desired for its own sake, he brought greater clarity to this Greek tradition. In beauty, the origin and end of existence— that is to say "the good"—is somehow also present even while remaining absent as origin and end. In this regard, beauty and the good are essentially the same. However, they differ with respect to how they present themselves to human thought and desire. The good that is sought as an end is present insofar as that end—whatever it may be—is conceived in its beauty, informing (as in putting its "form" "in") the one seeking it as an end.

Another contribution that Aristotle made was to recognize the way in which beauty involves a certain proportionality to human perception. "Beauty is a matter of size and order," he wrote, "and therefore becomes impossible in either a very minute creature . . . or in a creature of vast size."[7] This statement, and others like it,[8] is evidence that according to Aristotle, a thing's beauty can only be recognized if it is capable of being taken in by human perception.

It is important not to read Aristotle as an advocate for some sort of modern subjectivism, as if his statements assert that beauty is dependent upon a judgment of the mind. Rather, his view is much more practical: the beauty of a given entity can only be perceived to the extent that the given entity is itself perceivable; that is to say, a thing's beauty is bound up with its capacity to be perceived at all. If something is too small or too big its beauty cannot be

7. Aristotle, *Poetics*, 1451a.

8. E.g., in his *Rhetoric*, III, c.9 1409a, Aristotle contrasts a continuous writing style, which has no end in itself, with one more beautiful and pleasant because it has the beginning and end in itself and is thus limited to allow greater clarity for human understanding.

recognized. And no amount of subjective judgment can in reality declare a thing beautiful if that thing cannot be perceived in its integral wholeness. That is to say, beauty is in this respect far more dependent upon the real thing rather than the subjective perception of it, though Aristotle does provide room for a space between the two.

This chapter has sought to establish the origins of not only Christian reflection on beauty but also the association between beauty and God that comes to mark the Christian tradition. These origins reveal the primary roots of beauty as a power that calls, attracts, stirs wonder; as a plenitude of form; as perceivability and knowability; as something intelligible that exceeds normal modes of knowing; as something transcendent that descends upon reason and uplifts it; as an anagogical power; as closely related to love; as a causal force that shapes the world; as something that is desired in itself; and as appearing through a symmetry, proportion, or ordering of parts. As we will see, all of these continue to shape the Christian understanding of beauty as they are absorbed into the thinking and grammar of the early Church.

DISCUSSION QUESTIONS

1. How can the divine act of creation be understood as a "call"?

2. When viewed through the lens of beauty as a call, how might God's relationship to creation be understood?

3. In what ways does the ancient view of beauty differ from our late modern notions? In what ways might they be similar?

4. How are the human and the divine united in the phenomenon of beauty?

5. What are the primary contributions of the ancient Greek and Jewish perspectives for viewing God as beauty itself?

6. What sort of relationship can be found between beauty and the act of knowing in these primary ancient traditions?

2

THE BEAUTY OF GOD IN
THE EARLY CHURCH

As CHAPTER 1 EXPLAINED, it is not entirely incorrect to
say that for the ancient world beauty was in the eye of the
beholder. However, if the phrase "in the eye of the beholder" is taken for what it means today—that the individual
is the sole judge of what is or is not beautiful—then it is
anachronistic and invalid to apply it to the ancient world.
The ancient world simply did not emphasize the subjective
dimension of human existence in the way required for the
modern sense of that phrase to be meaningful. Nevertheless, since the ancient world conceived beauty in large
measure as the power within a thing to be perceivable and
knowable, it is valid to say that beauty was in the eye of
the beholder at all times: any given thing that can be seen,
known, and loved, derived this power from beauty. Beauty
was in the eyes of all beholders because beauty constituted

everything to which a person could be beholden. The modern phrase "in the eye of the beholder" is therefore an impoverishment of the much richer sense of beauty found in the ancient world.

The word "behold," and its cognates, is fitting: a percipient beholds something and in so doing is simultaneously "being held" by that thing—to "behold" is to "be" "held." The eye of the beholder is held in the thrall of the object upon which it gazes. The act of beholding identifies a two-way movement: both the movement of the percipient toward its perceived object, as well as the movement of the object itself toward its percipient. The word "behold" provides a fitting language to speak about beauty's call in an ancient world. Through the call of the cosmos for the Greeks and the call of God for the Jews, beauty not only attracted human persons to its manifold self-dispersion, but it came near to them.

Some time around what is now accepted to be about 4 BCE, however, Christians believe that beauty ruptured all limits and boundaries when it came as near to the world as it possibly could in the event of the Incarnation. In the theology of beauty it is precisely the Incarnation—the event wherein the God who creates enters into creation by assuming a human nature—that unlocked the mystery of beauty. It did so not by resolving beauty's complexities but rather by making beauty more visible than it had ever been or ever would be. Beauty and mystery were brought together in the person of Jesus Christ, whose life itself became the fullness of beauty. It was a beauty that transfigured mystery from a threatening unknown into an excess of knowable content, a person-centered surplus of intelligibility. As the twentieth-century French Jesuit Henri de Lubac once explained, "[t]he idea of mystery is perfectly acceptable once one has admitted the idea of a personal and transcendent God."[1] This is because once mystery is identifiable with something positive—such as a fullness of knowable content given by God—rather than something lacking that needs to be filled by human effort or something problematic that needs to be solved, mystery can be recognized as the very bond of love between persons. Only when God is believed to be both personal and transcendent can this idea of mystery become viable.

This chapter will explore the ways in which the Christ event, and the subsequent beginning of the Church, were themselves affected by and, in turn, contributed to the development of the theology of beauty. For almost the whole of the ancient world, beauty was an enigma, an intimidating unknown. Beauty harbored an ambiguity derived from the fact that the material entities through which beauty made itself present simultaneously pointed to a depth that transcended all material phenomena. With the Incarnation, the world was given a living principle by which both the material and the spiritual, the worldly and the other-worldly, were brought into harmony. In this way, the Incarnation became a concrete moment in which one of the primary principles of beauty—that beauty is a unity-in-plurality and hence a gathering power—was made manifest in the concrete fact of culture. Gathering goes hand in hand with ascent, since what is gathered is also transfigured anew, ennobled, or elevated into a greater good, in the community that results. The beauty that called to the ancient world, so it was believed, came near in the person of Jesus Christ as a power to gather a community to ascend ever higher into the divine life.

The Christ event, however, did not displace the pursuit of beauty that was launched in the Greek philosophical

1. Lubac, *Mystery of the Supernatural*, 171.

tradition. The Platonic-Aristotelian legacy endured not only in the academies where it continued to dwell, but also in the spawning of a new way of understanding Plato and Aristotle known today as Neoplatonism. As a hybrid of philosophical thought and religious sensibility, Neoplatonism not only attracted followers in its own right, but its language and grammar also became absorbed into the fledgling Church as a way to express Christianity's lofty mysteries. This chapter will also examine the developments in Neoplatonism in order to bring to visibility the contribution that this esteemed legacy bequeathed to the Christian theological tradition.

BEAUTY IN THE EARLY CHURCH: THE GATHERING I

The story of beauty in early Church begins with the attraction elicited by Jesus of Nazareth. It was an attraction, no doubt, shrouded in mystery but a mystery that provoked questions: Who is this man? Who is this person who attracts others? Who is this person whose words and deeds so intensely capture one's heart and mind? Who is this person who can perform such wonders as healing the blind, commanding the lame to walk, transforming water into wine? Who is this person who challenges both the Roman and the Jewish establishments and declares the poor to be the ones for whom the reign of God is intended? Who is this person who can pass through even the shadowy veil of death and return to continue to declare the good news of salvation? Indeed, who is this person who seems to command an authority only God could command? These and other questions were the almost necessary result of an encounter with a person who shattered all previous categories of knowledge and thought. They are questions that did not end with the gathering of the Church. Rather, they are questions that led only to more questions, enduring even today—they are questions that, in large measure, form the Church.

This attraction involved many layers ranging from the most superficial glance to the most intimate love. At the most superficial level, the existence of Jesus as an historical figure has always proven to hold a certain attraction for most people. Jesus' historical existence and the early origins of Christianity can be found in certain texts considered extra-canonical, or "outside the Church." Tacitus, Josephus, Pliny the Younger, and Seutonius, for instance, all provide evidence that something happened in the first century that was connected to someone called Jesus or Christ.[2] Being extra-canonical, these figures bear a certain degree of credibility to the late modern mind that believes a confessed commitment to something interferes with, rather than augments, knowledge of that thing.

Is there any way to know whether this attraction was unique? After all, several holy persons appeared on the scene during the first and second centuries. For instance, the story of Apollonius of Tyana is remarkable for how it parallels the life of Jesus: from the claim that he was conceived of supernatural means, to his itinerant preaching of the value of the spiritual over the material, to his gathering of disciples, to his miraculous healings, to the claim that he rose from the dead, to his own followers writing about him.[3] Surely figures such as this indicate that the attraction of Jesus was far from unique but was, in the constant cadence of modernity's mythology of its past, little more than the credulity of a world not yet enlightened to ways of science.

2. For one of the most recent accounts of the historical evidence for Jesus' existence, see Mykytiuk, "Did Jesus Exist?," 41–51, 76.

3. Ehrman, *Did Jesus Exist?*, 208–9.

One fact seems to undermine such reasoning: what has been gathered by Jesus Christ has not only endured, but has shaped the history of the world as it continues to ascend ever higher into new dimensions of its relationship with the divine. This most obvious fact, which is the most overlooked fact by critics of the Church and Christianity, merits profound consideration especially in relation to Apollonius and others like him. After all, where is the church of Apollonius of Tyana? Where is his legacy? What impact has he had upon societies and cultures, upon human creativity, upon how we understand the human person? It is hardly controversial to conclude that the attraction to Apollonius was simply not as powerful as the attraction to Jesus.

Indeed the whole story of the early Church can be read as a narrative of attraction to Jesus, and this way of reading puts beauty at center stage. To read the story of the Church as a narrative of beauty is not to deny the ecclesial intentionality of Jesus' mission, but rather to open the way to seeing this intentionality in the context of beauty. The twentieth-century Swiss Jesuit Hans Urs von Balthasar maintained that beauty can be understood as a natural form of faith.[4] What he meant is that the natural experiences that persons have with beauty parallel in important ways the experiences that believers have with faith. To put it another way, experiences of beauty transcend but do not exclude the categorical, conceptual, and analytical modes of knowing. Just like faith, beauty compels an assent beyond the sanction of the conscious will, beyond the authoritative consent of deliberative, or instrumental, rationality where consent derives from a complete grasp of that to which consent is being given. Experiences of beauty—just like the experience of faith—involve consenting to something

4. Balthasar, *The Glory of the Lord I: Seeing the Form*; see also García-Rivera, *The Garden of God: A Theological Cosmology*, c. 4.

that, although not understood fully, compels firm consent anyway. To put it more concisely, beauty, like faith, reveals a will beyond will, a desire for something one did not know she desired.

Both beauty and faith are made culturally and historically concrete in the person of Jesus Christ. The attraction that derived, and continues to derive, from his beauty, is also the origin of the faith that the Christian tradition maintains he alone can offer. The Christian Testament is replete with passages that encapsulate the idea of Jesus' beauty in a number of ways. It will be helpful to consider some of the more prominent of these.

The Life of Jesus

The two Evangelists who provide an account of his birth depict attraction to the infant Jesus amidst great tension. From Joseph's original anxiety about Mary's mysterious pregnancy, to the urgent need to travel for a census, to the overcrowded lodging that pushes Joseph and Mary to a stable, the arrival of Jesus, which is also the arrival of beauty into the world, happens against all expectations. In this sense, Jesus bears the Greek sense of beauty as *paraprosdokian*: that which surprises, or arrives against expectations, compelling those who witness it to reinterpret their original view of the event (as well as the whole of reality itself!).

The Gospel writers depict Jesus' public ministry in ways that further parallel other significant dimensions of beauty. Beginning with the way he calls his disciples, the Gospels identify Jesus as a person so attractive that the response of those called is immediate.[5] Von Balthasar's insight, noted above, is here brought further to light insofar as

5. Cf. Mark 1:20; 2:14; Matt 4:20; 9:9; Luke 5:11; John 1:37.

Jesus' call to faith, like beauty, provokes a sense of obedience beyond the conscious consent of the will. If it seems strange to associate obedience with beauty it is because we have come to believe that beauty is an attribute over which we ourselves have control; after all, if beauty is the eye of the beholder, it must obey me rather than vice versa.

However, beauty conceived as a "call" also means that beauty commands obedience. When most people today think of obedience, they think of consent that is independent of, or often contrary to, what they want. For this reason, obedience can often be discomforting. The kind of obedience commanded by beauty, however, is much different. Beauty commands a person to obey its self-offer in this sense: when something beautiful appears to a person, that person can do nothing except submit to beauty's arrival —an arrival that is often unexpected. In other words, the very perception of beauty in something beautiful is at the same time the revelation that one is attracted to something one does not fully know. Beauty pulls a person's desire out of an often dormant, unconscious state where beauty then excites desire, transforming it into the power of attraction. To put it simply, beauty presents to a person something that the person did not yet know she desired. To be sure, such a person remains free to resist the sort of obedience provoked by beauty. Such resistance, however, really becomes a resistance to oneself, a resistance to one's own capacity for beauty. In light of all this, it might be said that beauty gives not only what is obeyed, but also the power to obey it.

Jesus' attraction extends beyond those he calls, however. Throughout the Gospels, Jesus attracts throngs of crowds to himself. Most frequently these crowds are drawn into listening to his words.[6] But there are times where Jesus

6. Cf. Matt 4:24–25; 7:28; 9:33; 21:45–46; Mark 3:7; 6:33; 8:1; Luke 2:8, 46–47.

provokes the attraction of aversion or hatred.[7] Hatred is, after all, a form of attraction, only an attraction that wills disintegration rather than integration and that results in discord or dissonance, as the medieval theologian Thomas Aquinas maintained.[8] This is why it is often said that indifference rather than hatred is the opposite of love; indifference is the absence of any attraction whatsoever. If there is one overarching theme that seems to run throughout the Christian Testament texts (as well as the history of the Western world), it is that one may love or hate Jesus Christ, but one cannot remain indifferent to him.

Not only is Jesus attractive in himself, his words and his teachings can be read as extensions of his beauty. His whole pedagogy, or "teaching philosophy," revolves around the kind of intelligibility communicated through parables, stories designed to communicate higher truths through the everyday events familiar to listeners. There is a sense in which parables were used not only to communicate a higher truth, but to hide or conceal it in order to draw one in and provoke her to a deeper sense of wonder. Parables, then, bear the stamp of that Greek sense of the *anagogical* element of beauty: that feature of beauty that uplifts the intellect in an act of spiritual ascent. It is true that there were times where his teaching tended more toward an engagement with the written form of his Jewish tradition.[9] Even here, however, he adorned these traditional statutes with flourishes that provoke attraction and response, whether of love or hatred.

Jesus did not heal or perform miracles for the spectacle of it, though their becoming a spectacle always remained a

7. Luke 4:28–30; Mark 6:3–4; Matt 13:57–58.

8. Thomas Aquinas, *Summa Theologiae* I-II, 29, 1.

9. Cf. Matt 4:14–17; 15:7–9; 21:42; 22:37; Mark 7:6; 10:3–9; Luke 4: 8–13; etc.

risk. Instead, the deeper truth that these miracles intended to communicate was the same truth communicated in his parables: that in and through Jesus Christ the Kingdom of God is at hand. Beauty always risks attracting a person only to the surface level appearance of the beautiful object. Content with the surface, the person would cease to go any deeper into the beautiful object, and therefore would cease ascending into the depths that beauty communicates. In a similar way, a faith that remains only at the surface level of Jesus' miracles or parables also ceases to ascend into the depths of divine content they intend. This is why the beauty that Jesus communicates is everywhere shrouded in mystery. It seems that faith and miracles do not seek merely to disseminate some separable fact of God, or some divine information to be used as humans want. Rather, what is intended in all this is a relationship, and nothing engenders relationship more than the mystery and attraction of beauty. Without this, without something more to be known that attracts a person who desires to know, there can be no relationship.

So the perpetual attraction elicited by beauty means that the relationship it engenders is always ascending. This notion is perhaps most poignantly captured in one of the most significant accounts of beauty in the Gospels, namely, Jesus' transfiguration. This event, recorded in three of the four Gospels[10] and alluded to in one of the general epistles (2 Pet 1:16–18) and more loosely in John's Gospel (John 1: 14), depicted what is believed to be the culmination of Jesus' public life. Taking Peter, James, and John, Jesus ascended to the top of Mt. Tabor where "his face did shine as the sun, and his garments did become white as snow." On either side of Jesus appeared both Elijah and Moses, representing prophecy and law. Along with the voice of

10. Matt 17:1–6; Mark 9:1–8; Luke 9:28–36.

God, there were three heavenly witnesses (Elijah, Moses, and God) and three earthly witnesses (Peter, James, and John), satisfying the Deuteronomic requirement that there be three witnesses to testify to any fact (Deut 19:15).

In this event, however, there were three witnesses in heaven and three on earth, testifying to the fact that Jesus stands in between heaven and earth, arguably mediating the two. The themes of ascent and light, which are significant with respect to the tradition of beauty, represent here a divine glory that breaks through the material order to show itself in order to uplift the earthly into the heavenly. What is most important for our purposes, however, concerns Peter's suggestion to build shelters for Elijah, Moses, and Jesus. In the midst of the event, Peter's suggestion—that is to say, his desire to contain the glory that he is privileged to witness—falls on deaf ears. The theological point here seems to be that the beauty that shines in Christ is not meant to be contained or enshrined but rather heard and imitated. The voice from the cloud says to the three earthly witnesses, "this is my beloved son with whom I am well pleased. Listen to him." Sheltering the two heavenly witnesses along with Christ would cease any ascent into the light of divine glory that the event seems to intend.

Indeed, the tension between continuing to ascend with Christ into the light of divine glory and enshrining him in our desire for shelter became one of the perpetual challenges the Church continually seems to face. Especially today, Christians of all kinds find themselves tempted to build "shelters" in the glory that Christ alone can give, whether those shelters take the form of a political ideology, a moral stance, or simply an unhealthy spiritual or physical desire. But the beauty of Christ continues to bear in itself the power to allow one to hear the voice say, "this is my beloved son with whom I well pleased. Listen to *him*." Shelters may provide temporary comfort, but they only inhibit the ascent into divine glory that God intends and for which hope endures.

The Pashcal Mystery

The culmination of the mystery of Jesus Christ, that is to say the most intense concretion of Jesus' beauty, is what has traditionally been called the Paschal Mystery. This identifies the mystery of Jesus' suffering that begins with the cross on Good Friday, endures through Holy Saturday when it is believed Jesus' descends into Hell, and climaxes with Jesus' resurrection from the dead on Easter Sunday. This culmination of Jesus' life and mission is also the culmination of his beauty insofar as it is the apex of not only his gathering power but also his anagogical power. If Jesus' earthly ministry sought to gather all people into his Church, the Paschal Mystery constitutes the moment when this gathering transcends the limits of the earthly, material order gathering even those who have gone before.

How is it possible to speak of the beauty of the crucifixion, an event that bore witness to the ugliness of violence, of sin, of a humanity that has rejected God, of the most innocent suffering? Again, it is important to remember that beauty in this sense is not simply outward adornment or prettiness, but the power at the very origin of all existence to call, attract, and gather together. The beauty of the cross, however, cannot stand by itself but can only be seen in the light of the resurrection. And before the resurrection there is the beauty of Holy Saturday when Christ descended into Hell.

His descent into Hell marks a moment when Jesus' beauty, that is to say his embodiment of that power which calls to all creatures, goes so far as to radiate that call even to those who have rejected it the first time around. In this sense, Jesus' descent into Hell reveals the way in which divine beauty is an excess of attraction. It does not abide a limit, not even the limits of personal refusal. It does not transgress those limits against one's individual will, to be sure, but nor does it acquiesce to them. Rather, as Jesus' descent into Hell seems to reveal, beauty's perpetual call, its constant attraction, goes as far as it can to pull the obstinate will out of its self-imposed alienation without dishonoring that will in its integrity.

The resurrection marks the moment at which beauty's power comes into its fullest manifestation as it calls to all people. Whether this call is met with rejection or acceptance, it is heard and continues to be heard throughout the world. For those who accept it as revealed truth, the call issued by the resurrection gathers together the Church. The Apostle Paul believed that the resurrection was the *sine qua non* of the Christian faith, so much so that if it did not take place, then, as he wrote, "our faith is in vain" (1 Cor 15:14). As the reality of the Church verifies, there has been and continues to be a multitude of people who have heard and have responded to the call echoing from the empty tomb. In light of Paul's comment, then, it could be said that the resurrection is the call that founds the Church.

Furthermore, the resurrection reveals an excess of intelligible content, so much so that it explodes every means that we have for trying to render its content conceivable. In order for things or events to be conceived, they must somehow conform to finite minds. But what happens when a thing or event simply does not fit into the categories or concepts used by these finite minds? Most often, it enters into a less standard, artistic/poetic economy of communication, giving birth to beautiful works of art. It can also give birth to new categories or concepts, which can then be applied to repeated instances of the original event. In part, this is what happens with the resurrection. Except, not only does the resurrection give birth to a new "category" for understanding the world, namely, Christianity, it also reveals the limits of every category and concept that humans construct—including Christianity itself! At its heart, Christianity is a personal relationship. Hence, Christianity must be *practiced*, *must be lived*, rather than merely serve as a category or concept. Indeed, Christianity only really makes sense as a category for thinking and loving the world when it is practiced and lived. This is arguably the most important dimension of the "foundation" established by the resurrection.

BEAUTY IN PAUL: THE GATHERING II

The Apostle Paul, known as "the apostle to the Gentiles," plays a significant role in the divine act of gathering for two reasons. First, Paul did not know Jesus during his lifetime. He is believed to have encountered the risen Christ on the road to Damascus. Yet, despite this, his influence and his leadership in establishing a number of Churches are remarkable. Second, as the apostle to the Gentiles, Paul is a figure through whom the Word opened and extended itself beyond the limits of the Jewish communities. His teaching as a whole is rich and complex and it bears immense significance for understanding the way in which the tradition of beauty before him enters more fully into the early Christian communities.[11] For the sake of brevity, however, we will examine only those teaching that are most relevant to beauty.

11. For some of the best theological work on Paul, see Wright, *What Saint Paul Really Said*; and Matera, *God's Saving Grace: A Pauline Theology*.

By far the most significant contribution that Paul makes to the role and place of beauty in the early Church is his letter to the Romans, which was not only his longest and most theologically complex letter, but also, according to most scholars, his last letter. The Church in Rome, just like Rome itself, was a community mixed with Jews and Gentiles, which made it necessary for Paul to address certain aspects of the Law given to the Jews. Although this is a highly complex area of his thought, it becomes possible to discern how his approach contributed to the already growing tradition of beauty in the early Church.

First, the law communicates an excess of intelligible content. It conveys prohibitions, to be sure, and these are clearly conceivable. However, for Paul, the law also bears the power to elevate consciousness into the depths of the intelligibility it conveys by making human beings aware of sin. In this sense, the law is *anagogical* as it enables intellectual and spiritual ascent where one's capacity to see sinfulness becomes clearer and clearer. But this ascent does not, of itself, perform the positive function of leading a person into the freedom that God intends. Such freedom can only come from the faith that, as Paul maintained, "comes through hearing" (Rom 10:17). So the law, from this perspective, by elevating a person's consciousness of sin also opens one's ears to a better capacity to hear. And what is it that is heard but the very call of God toward a more profound union with Him; what is heard is the divine attractiveness, that is, Beauty itself.

So a second dimension of what might be called Paul's theology of beauty involves the notion of hearing this call. But where the tradition that preceded him could only ever hear the distant echo of this call, for Paul, Christ is the call at its most intense sounding. Christ precisely is the excess of intelligibility that the law had always already sought to communicate, or perhaps anticipated. This is why Christ's presence and the faith he offers does not do away with the law completely, but rather fulfills it, directs it into the freedom it had always intended. The faith given in and through Christ, rather than "nullifying the law . . . upholds the law" as Paul explained to the Church in Rome (3:31).

A second important element of what could be called Paul's nascent theology of beauty, more philosophical in nature, concerns the relationship between the universal and the particular (Rom 1:1–6; 14–16). For Paul, salvation through the Jews and the law is universally intended, that is, intended for all humankind. This universality, however, is made known to the world through the particular history of the Jewish people through whom God communicates it. Most significantly, it is made known through the particular life of Jesus Christ, in whom Christians believe God himself entered history and lived a particular, concrete life. Accordingly, the universality of sin and the need for salvation is communicated through the particularity of the law. And so where many might tend to see the universal and the particular as little more than opposites, Paul sees a symbiotic relationship. This kind of thinking became a staple of not only Pauline theology, but of Christianity in general, enabled as it was by the Incarnation and the principles that flow from Beauty.

Perhaps the most significant example of Paul's theology of beauty is found in the way in which it enabled him to view the relationship between the spiritual and the material, and therefore the relationship between God and the world. Recall again how in chapter 1 we saw the limits of ancient Greek rationality to finally mediate between the spiritual and the material. Thinking in the light of the Incarnation, Paul is able to overcome such limits and say, "For the invisible things of him [God] since the creation of the world are clearly seen, being perceived through the things that are made, even his everlasting power and divinity. . ." (Rom 1:20). The significance of this verse for the tradition of Christian beauty cannot be overstated.

As a principle, Romans 1:20 gave verbal form to the idea that God's "being" is so beyond all things that it alone can indwell them *most intimately* (as later theologians would explain). It also brought spiritual depth and material surface together such that both could be unified—without becoming blurred—under the name "beauty." Such a notion relieved the tension that the Greeks saw so clearly since, with Paul, beauty could be seen to indwell all beautiful things without blurring the distinction necessary for such indwelling in the first place. Paul's insight held that the divine presence is in all things in such a way as to avoid compromising either God's transcendence or the unique integrity of creatures.

It was an insight that at once invested all things in the world with a divine value, without falling into the trap of pantheism. Consequently, as the sixth-century Eastern theologian Dionysius the Areopagite would come to assert, all things could become a help to contemplating God.[12] This meant, further, that the world, both in its natural and its artificial (i.e., humanly constructed) state, were no longer necessarily prisons to be escaped, as so much of the ancient world believed. Rather, the world could now be seen as a communication from God, albeit, since the world is fallen, a communication through a glass darkly (cf. 1 Cor 13:12). In Paul, the Incarnation was more than an historical event. It was itself a truth so real that it penetrated to the very heart of how he saw the world. It was a way of seeing, of thinking, of believing, wherein difference served unity and unity expressed itself in difference.

12. Dionysius the Areopagite, *Celestial Hierarchy*, ch. 2, section 4.

BEAUTY IN NEOPLATONISM

As the Church was beginning to take shape in the ancient world, Greek philosophy was undergoing its own spiritual revival. Plato's legacy continued to exercise significant influence among the educated classes throughout the Mediterranean region. Plato's philosophy had always harbored a certain mystical flavor insofar as it sought to elevate the intellect into the higher realm of ideas. It was not explicitly religious, to be sure, primarily because "the religious" had not yet become a definable characteristic or category as we know it to be today. Nevertheless, as Platonic thought developed it soon encountered the fledgling Church, whose influence upon it became substantial.

Under the guidance of the third-century figure Plotinus (AD 204–270), Platonism absorbed many of the spiritual ideas and impulses born from Christianity and other forces giving rise to what is now known as Neoplatonism. As an interpretation of Plato's thought, Neoplatonism bore the stamp of its namesake; however it did so in the light of several novel developments. And inasmuch as influence is never a one-way street, Neoplatonism exercised significant impact upon the developing Church. One of the most poignant points of influence concerned the way in which Neoplatonism provided to early Christian thinkers a way of understanding and speaking about beauty and its relation to God.

From the third century under Plotinus, to the fifth century under Proclus (AD 412–85)—a figure who is known as the last of the Neoplatonists—the Greek understanding of beauty received some significant insights. Plotinus is perhaps best known for recognizing the way in which the classical Greek notion that beauty is symmetry points to a "something more" beyond that symmetry. If it is true that a thing is beautiful because it bears a symmetry of parts, then it follows, Plotinus thought, that each of these parts themselves must also be beautiful.[13] But if beauty derives *only* from a symmetry of parts, then it would follow that nothing single or simple without symmetry, such as those parts constituting a whole, can be beautiful. And if the parts cannot be beautiful then it follows that the whole cannot be beautiful, and the whole theory of symmetry falls apart.

In order to fully appreciate the ramifications of Plotinus's insight, it is necessary to first understand the general components of his philosophy of being. Like almost all Greek philosophers from Plato onward, Plotinus believed that the source of all being, of all that is, was, and will be, was the One. It was an accepted philosophical principle that every multitude must derive from a prior unity. Now, everything in the world constitutes a cosmic multitude, which means that the source of this multitude must be a unity, pure and perfect. The One identifies such a unified source. But in order for this One to truly be a One, it can have absolutely no relation to any other whatsoever. To even "think" the One is to put oneself into relation with it and thus compromise its oneness in some way. Obviously, this makes attempting to articulate anything about the One paradoxical if not impossible.

It would not be accurate to identify the One as the god of Neoplatonism, since the notion of a god in Greek thought differed in significant ways from what it becomes in Christianity. The Greeks still had their gods, who were all particular instances of the category "god." And the category "god" differed in significant ways from the notion of a philosophical principle, which as such were more primordial than even the gods. Understood from this perspective, the One was a non-personal principle, a source or cause

13. Plotinus, *Enneads*, bk. 1, chapter 6, section 1.

of all existence. And unlike the God of Christianity, the One's causal activity was not viewed as a freely willed act of love, but an overflow of its fullness from which emanates all existence. Here is how Plotinus describes it: "This we may say is the first act of generation: the One, perfect because it seeks nothing, has nothing, and needs nothing, overflows, as it were, and its superabundance makes something other than itself."[14]

That which comes into being from this act of emanation is necessarily constituted by a lack of the One's fullness. But it turns back toward the One and in so doing begins to fill its lack. It does not become another One, but rather becomes a knowing of the One that makes it Intellect or *nous* in Greek terminology. As Intellect, or *nous*, this emanation is now a two rather than a one: in being emanated it is existence, and in its turning back to the One it is intellect. In this duality, *nous* embodies the actuality and potentiality of all existence, which means that *nous* is the being and knowing of all that is, was, and will be. So what does all this have to do with beauty?

Even though it is not without ambiguity—which is not surprising given that his thinking derives from the earlier Greek doctrine of beauty—the theory of Plotinus identifies *nous*, rather than the One, with beauty. And in so doing, he configures beauty as the first emanation rather than the origin itself. This is significant since Christianity will go further than Neoplatonism to identify God's very self with beauty, as we will see. Nevertheless, Plotinus makes some significant contributions to this Christian development.

As noted already, Plotinus identified beauty with the whole of existence, that is, *nous* in its emanated state. But beauty was also an intellectual principle, a fullness of all that can be intelligible, that is, *nous* in its turning back to

14. Plotinus, *Enneads*, bk. 5, ch. 2, sect. 1.

the One. As the fullness of all intelligible content, beauty in Plotinus was pushed further between the material and the spiritual, bearing a significant intellectual dimension. Furthermore, because *nous* was the fullness of all that is, beauty was a unity-in-plurality, thus giving philosophic formulation to Paul's Incarnational theology. Plotinus also advanced the idea that beauty is not only identifiable as a symmetry of parts, but also the simplicity or unity behind such symmetry. In this way, he opened the doors for identifying God, who is without parts and supremely simple, with beauty itself.

The Neoplatonic legacy would endure for a few more centuries until Emperor Justinian officially closed the Platonic Academy in 529. The last of the great Neoplatonic thinkers was Proclus of Athens, whose contribution to the understanding of beauty and its relation to the supreme principle was significant for a few reasons. First, where his predecessors had focused on the supreme principle itself (the One) and *nous*, Proclus focused upon the desire or longing that bonds these, namely, *eros*. In his account, *eros* is the eternal longing that draws beings back toward the One, which means that *eros* is also the very presence of the One in things. It is not an identical presence, since this would compromise the absolute unity of the One, but rather a derived or secondary presence. But with even this secondary presence, the identification of *nous* as beauty took a step further toward the One. In so doing, it enabled two important principles: (1) insofar as *eros* emanates from the One, it identifies a causal power that became associated with beauty; and (2) not only was beauty identified with the fullness of all intelligible content as *nous*, it was also associated with the *eros* that brought *nous* back toward the One. This step further developed the philosophical foundations for the identification between beauty and primary causality, on the one hand, and between beauty and love, on the other hand. As we will see, both of these dimensions of beauty become significant themes in the Christian tradition.

DISCUSSION QUESTIONS

1. How does the Christ event, the life of Jesus, advance many of the themes of beauty as found in the ancient Greek and Jewish traditions?

2. How might viewing the formation of the early Church through the lens of beauty provide unique resources for viewing the role of Church in the world today?

3. In what ways does looking at the life of Christ from the tradition of beauty draw out aspects of his life that might be otherwise overlooked?

4. How does Jesus, as God incarnate, reinforce the idea that God is beauty itself?

5. How can the theology of St. Paul be seen as a merger of both the Greek and Jewish traditions of beauty?

6. What important developments of the ancient Greek understanding of beauty can be found in the Neoplatonic approach to beauty?

3

GIVING GOD THE NAME BEAUTY

"What's in a name? That which we call a rose by any other name would smell as sweet." These famous lines from Shakespeare's *Romeo and Juliet* are often quoted by those who argue, with Juliet, that names of things are not important. Rather, what is important is *what things are*. The irony of these lines ought not be taken for granted. Juliet's words are really a plea that Romeo's name, which marks him as an enemy to Juliet's house, not interfere with their love affair. As is well known, the results of the story seem to stand in stark contrast to the belief behind Juliet's plea.

It seems we simply cannot escape names, not only because it is only through names that we identify *what things are* but also because all words, in some sense, are really names. This does not mean that names are all we have, but rather that it is important to recognize both the *unity and distinction* between names and what they identify.

Reflection upon the relationship between a name and that which it identifies did not originate in Shakespeare's day, but rather has a long philosophical history stretching back to the ancient Greeks. Plato was one of the first to philosophically inquire into this relationship and the results of his inquiry can be found in his dialogue *The Cratylus*. Aristotle addressed several dimensions of this relationship in works such as his *Posterior Analytics*, *Topics*, and *On Interpretation*. Scholars in the Middle Ages would distinguish a *res significata* (the thing signified) from the *modus significandi* (way of signifying, i.e., a name), recognizing both their unity and their difference. In the modern period, Ludwig Wittgenstein believed that by examining the logic underlying the relationship between language and the world he could resolve a great many philosophical problems. Today, it is common for universities to have a department of linguistics tasked with studying the nature of language, what it reveals about human nature, and how it allows human beings to relate to the world.

In this chapter, we will examine beauty and the nature of theological language by inquiring how beauty became a name for God. The primary figure responsible for this naming was the ancient figure Dionysius the Areopagite, whose own name and identity, as we will see, are not without controversy. As can already be discerned, Dionysius entered into a long tradition that had in many ways at least gestured toward naming God "Beauty." As the early Church grew and flourished, the theology of beauty latent in the gospel and in Paul was further nourished by theologians from the second to the sixth centuries, most of whom were influenced by Neoplatonism. Among these was the greatest theologian of the Latin West, Augustine of Hippo, who made significant contributions to the development of the Christian theology of beauty. We will begin this chapter by looking to him first before moving on to our main figure, Dionysius the Areopagite.

AUGUSTINE OF HIPPO

Aurelius Augustinus (AD 354–429) lived a life that was surprisingly similar to many of today's young adults. Born in the town of Thagaste in the North African Province of Numidia, in what is today Algeria, his mother Monica had converted to Christianity and lived a very pious life, and his father Patricius was a Roman pagan who converted on his death bed. Like many young people today, Augustine was given the opportunity of an education and showed himself to be intellectually gifted. Like many young people today, Augustine also demonstrated a deep passion and desire for the sensual side of life. In the well-known phrase, his early adulthood was a life of wine, women, and song. In his *Confessions*—an unprecedented literary work, which was the first in the ancient world to combine theology and philosophy in a journey of deep, personal introspection—he often recounts how his youth was full of lust and desires for the flesh.[1] So we have in Augustine a figure in whom the battle between a brilliant intellect and insatiable desire led to a knowledge of God that was as intimate, heartfelt, and personal as it was intellectual, contemplative, and reflective. His journey to greatness, however, was anything but smooth, a fact that he recounts with joy in his *Confessions*

1. See, e.g., *Confessions* bk. 2, ch. 2, section 1: "puberty . . . the broiling sea of my fornication. . ."; bk. 2, ch. 2, section, 3; "This was the age at which a frenzy gripped me and I surrendered myself completely to lust. . ."; bk. 3, ch. 1, section 1: "I went to Carthage where I found myself in a hissing cauldron of lust."

as he saw God working through every stumbling block that beset him.

Early in his education, at the age of sixteen, he sought to use his intellectual gifts in the pursuit of political power. He set off for Carthage to study the art of rhetoric (persuasive speech) in hopes of becoming a politician. Although his mother had already converted to Christianity, its call to him would remain during these years but a distant echo. Instead, he felt himself drawn to the teachings of a cult called Manichaeism. This cult believed that there were ultimately two forces that had created the world: a force of light, or good, that created spirit, and a force of darkness, or evil, that created matter. This teaching and others flowing from it attracted Augustine because he believed it could resolve the problem of evil. As he continued his studies, however, his encounter with the Neoplatonism of Plotinus and another later Neoplatonist by the name of Porphyry (AD 234–305) would compel him to abandon his Manichaeism, but it would take another twelve years or so before he was finally rid of it. Throughout all this, as he tells us in his *Confessions*, he felt an ever-increasing restlessness in his heart that seemed less and less capable of being stilled by his own pursuits. As he famously remarks, "You have made us for yourself, Oh Lord, and our hearts are restless until they rest in you."[2]

Eventually Augustine became a teacher of rhetoric and moved to Milan, where he would visit the cathedral to hear Ambrose, Bishop of Milan, preach on Christianity as a way of life. Ambrose proved himself to be a very persuasive rhetorician, which attracted Augustine who had developed a love for the art of words. After some time, however, Augustine found himself being opened, not so much by Ambrose's words themselves, but their content. Augustine saw

2. Augustine, *Confessions*, bk. 1, ch. 1, section 1.

the beauty in Christianity, as its truth penetrated to the very depths of his restless heart, stilling it in ways nothing else had been able to. A well-known story recounts a momentous day in Augustine's life. He was sitting in a garden in Milan when he heard some children singing *tolle lege, tolle lege*, or "take and read, take and read." He interpreted these words as a divine instruction to "take and read" Paul's letter to the Romans, which he had been holding in his hand. Reading Paul's words three centuries after Paul had written them, Augustine tells of how he was seized by a great light. Contrary to what Manichaeism had taught him, he saw in Christianity as presented by Paul a beauty in the material world that had eluded him. He also saw how the One God of all could be present in the things of the world, communicating his divine beauty in and through daily activities. At that moment the scales fell from his eyes as tears flowed freely. On April 25, 387, he was baptized into the Church in the very cathedral where he had so often heard Ambrose preach.

Augustine is most well-known for what might be called his political theology—depicted in his famous work *The City of God*—but his theology is everywhere driven by beauty. Under the influence of Pauline theology and Neoplatonic thought, beauty became for Augustine a significant theme for his theological project. Of course, it would not have taken much for this theme to resonate with him, given his deep sense of yearning and desire, his attraction to the world, to philosophy and the intellectual life. His draw to "wine, women, and song" was provoked and sustained, as he would later reflect, by the beauty he saw there. It was through this beauty that he would come to understand God calling to him.

It is in light of this call through the beauty of the world that Augustine registers one of his famous lines: "Late have I loved you, Beauty so old and so new: late have I loved you."[3] Augustine is here addressing God by the name Beauty and recognizing its eternal character. After his conversion, Augustine came to see how God was in fact present in all the different beautiful entities that attracted him. Through both St. Paul and the Neoplatonic thinkers, he was able to recognize this feature of beauty that had escaped his notice. He also understood the way in which all the beautiful things in the world that attracted him compelled him to offer his love to them. "My weight is my love," he wrote, "and by this I am taken wherever I am taken."[4] For Augustine the allure of beauty and the power of desire was more than a fleeting experience; it was something that shapes who we become and how we relate to the world, others, and God. Augustine believed that in giving ourselves to these beautiful things we become who we are, which is to say we find ourselves in the beauty that draws us. For this reason, he would go so far as to say "Since love grows within you, so beauty grows. For love is the beauty of the soul."[5] In other words, beauty takes the form of love within the soul, which indicates the kinship—even parity—between beauty and love. Augustine would have encountered the idea of their proximity in both biblical and Neoplatonic sources. It could be argued that the above insight, along with another of his famous doctrines, namely, "we are only able to love what is beautiful,"[6] demonstrates the way that he identified beauty and love. For if love is the beauty of the soul, and if we are only able to love what is beautiful, then beauty is love made visible in the external world around us.

3. Augustine, *Confessions*, bk. 10, ch. 27, section 38.

4. Augustine, *Confessions*, bk. 13, ch. 9, section 10.

5. Augustine, *Homilies on the First Epistle of John*, Ninth Homily, section 9.

6. Augustine, *On Music*, bk. 6, ch. 13, section 20.

And so Augustine was stirred to wonder, "are things beautiful because we love them, or do we love them because they are beautiful?" In other words, does something become beautiful simply because I desire it? Or is my desire provoked by beautiful things that draw me outside myself? It is a question that today might be characterized as inquiring whether beauty is "objective" or "subjective"; that is, is beauty in the eye of the beholder such that we control its appearance, or is beauty something that calls us out of ourselves toward something greater than ourselves? For Augustine, reflecting back upon the way in which his desire for beauty led him to love the God who is "Beauty so old and so new," the answer was clear: beauty calls us.

Stressing the anagogical power of beauty, Augustine understood how, even though our desires erupt from within, they are bidden by something from beyond ourselves. This does not mean that Augustine did not appreciate the way in which beauty works in the personal experience of the individual. The fact that beauty calls to us, rather than being controlled by us, in no way committed Augustine to a position that flattens each person's experience of beauty to the same. Following the Neoplatonic doctrine that beauty identifies a unity-in-plurality, Augustine maintained that the unity of all disparate entities in which beauty appears is the form of beauty. That is to say, beauty's unity requires the diversity of its many appearances. Otherwise, unity is reduced to uniformity and, if everything is the same, there is no beauty.

Given his early place in the canon of Christian thinkers, there was only so much that Augustine could do with respect to the role of beauty within the theological tradition. Living in the twilight of the Roman Empire, his was a time of great political upheaval, and most of his theological energies were ordered toward the relationship between the growing Church and the social order. Nevertheless, the burgeoning tradition of theological beauty can still claim this great Western Father of the Church as one of its primary pillars especially for the ways he advanced many of the prior notions of beauty. Most importantly, he addressed God as Beauty itself, bearing this important theme into Western posterity.

DIONYSIUS THE AREOPAGITE—AN "UNKNOWN MONK"

Dionysius the Areopagite was believed to have been a firsthand witness to St. Paul's teachings. In chapter seventeen of the *Acts of the Apostles*, one finds an account of Paul preaching to a group of philosophers in Athens, at a place called the Areopagus. Paul explains how he saw their deep religious sensibilities as he walked through their city, including an altar with the inscription that read "to an unknown god." In response, Paul proclaimed the God "who made the world and everything in it, who is Lord of heaven, who does not live in shrines made by human hands . . . the God in whom we live and move and have our being," and who will judge the world in righteousness through the man whom God raised from the dead. The passage ends at verse thirty-four, which reads: "But some of them joined him and became believers, including Dionysius the Areopagite. . ."

For a great part of the Christian tradition, this figure was believed to have written a small collection of treatises covering a number of theological themes. Because he had been converted to Christianity after hearing Paul preach first hand, his thoughts and ideas caught the attention of some of the greatest minds in the Christian tradition. It might be surprising, then, to learn that this figure remains unknown even to this day. Why is this so?

Sometime around the mid-fifth century, during the height of ecclesial debates concerning the nature of Jesus Christ, a group involved in the debate brought forth a collection of texts that bore the signature Dionysius the Areopagite. Immediately they were met with suspicion since no *known* theological authority prior to this appearance had mentioned this figure in any work. Nevertheless, the contents of these texts, along with the belief that their author was the figure converted by St. Paul at the Areopagus, were able to persuade most to their authenticity, and their influence was equally immediate.

It was in fact the contents of the collection of these texts fortified by the alleged eyewitness authority of their author that sustained their authority for the next twelve hundred years or so. The authority of Dionysius reached its pinnacle among the theologians of the Middle Ages, who drew from the Dionysian well a number of different theological principles, doctrines, and ideas. By the time the texts were organized and housed at the University of Paris around the close of the first millennium, they consisted of four primary works—*On the Divine Names*, *Celestial Hierarchy*, *Ecclesial Hierarchy*, and *Mystical Theology*—along with eleven epistles. Interest in these writings generated a formidable commentary tradition within the medieval world that included contributions from a number of scholars. It was not until the sixteenth century, around the time when the first organized editions of these texts were being published, that the authorship of these texts were once again met with suspicion by humanists like Lorenzo Valla and Erasmus of Rotterdam. Martin Luther added to the controversy by recommending that Christians "shun like the plague" the contents of these mystical writings because Dionysius "Platonizes more than he Christianizes." Nevertheless, other scholars like Marsilio Ficino remained convinced of the authentic identity of the author and worked tirelessly to prove it.

Toward the end of the nineteenth century, when the editions of these texts were being critically examined, two German philologists, Josef Stiglmayr and Hugo Koch, investigated certain dimensions internal to the writings of Dionysius. Based upon the presence in the Dionysian text of a liturgical form that dated only to the fifth century in Syria, as well as similarities between passages in the text with passages found in Proclus, they were able to determine that the authorship could not have occurred before the sixth century. The resulting consensus was that Dionysius the Areopagite was a name chosen by an author who was most likely a monk living in the Eastern Roman Empire, probably in or near Syria, who lived during the late fifth, or early sixth century. These discoveries ushered in a new wave of Dionysian scholarship, whose task it was to learn why the author would claim the name he did.

Some of the more skeptical responses sought to dismiss the texts as nothing but the products of a forger falsely claiming to be a biblical eyewitness in order to bolster his credibility. By the late twentieth century, however, this became something of a fringe position. Most scholars set themselves to the task of understanding why the name from Acts 17:34 was chosen and what it meant for the texts. These scholars rejected the notion, advanced by skeptics, that the sole reason these texts had proven so influential was due to the identity of their author. Such a claim, they argued, not only neglected the way in which the contents of these writings had corresponded to a great deal in the Christian tradition, even providing important connections between schools of thought, but it also misconstrued the significance of an authoritative name.

From its beginning the Christian theological tradition had been wary of false teachings, as the history of heresy shows. Simply possessing the name of a biblical eyewitness would not have been enough to secure any significant degree of theological authority. Only if the contents of any given writing proved to be consistent with the developing tradition would an authoritative name connected to that writing bear any weight. In light of this position, a new community of scholars arose around what was now an unknown author with a collection of texts that had proven immensely influential within the developing Christian theological tradition.

NAMING GOD?

As already noted, among the works of Dionysius is a text called *On the Divine Names*. In the Christian theological tradition, it is the first treatise to systematically propose and examine a set of names attributed to God, though it is not without precedent.

In the Jewish tradition, as we saw in chapter 1, Moses asked God for a name to present to the Israelites. God obliged with both *HaShem* (YHWH) and *Ehyeh Asher Ehyeh*, both of which identify the divine unboundedness and absolute faithfulness. These names in the Jewish sense intended to communicate the intimacy between God and his chosen people. Some of the Cappadocian Fathers—theologians living in the fourth century, in a region called Cappadocia—made references to certain divine names in treatises whose main theme was to counter certain heresies. But these cannot be considered systematic treatises on the divine names (and it is worth noting that the name Beauty is not among those listed).

So what exactly does Dionysius mean by a "divine name"? Dionysius firmly adhered to the Jewish notion that God is unbounded faithfulness and generosity. God's "being"—which for Dionysius is not a proper reference for God since God is even beyond "being" insofar as our use of this name necessarily implies a category—is the unlimited excess of all being and kinds of being. This is what it means to say, as Dionysius does, that God is perfect, superessential, being: there is nothing lacking in God, nothing outside of God after which God's essence must strive to become complete. God is the giver of all that is, was, and will be and so infinitely beyond all these. Due to its excessive surplus, God's perfection is given in diverse ways, so that one may say there are many divine perfections that are given to creatures to help them become more "perfect," that is, more fully complete in their existence. The divine names identify these perfections.

To put it concisely, a divine name is a perfection of God that proceeds from his unlimited excess of being and enters into the order of creation by constituting at their inmost depths the formal properties of all beings. As stated in the introduction, a divine name can be considered God's public identity in contrast with God's more intimate identity as it is given in the various faith traditions. These names include: good, light, beauty, love, truth, being, wisdom, life, virtue, almighty, ancient of days, perfect, and one. As names of God, these perfections identify God insofar as God communicates his Being in and as creation. For Dionysius, God's essence in itself is forever hidden and remains completely incomprehensible to human beings not on account of God's incapacity to communicate it, but on account of the human being's incapacity to receive it. The divine essence in itself, in other words, is simply too immense, too great to be taken in by the finite intellect. As

Aristotle had explained centuries before, there is no proportion between the finite and the infinite.[7] This is why God communicates himself through his names: since his essence cannot be received, God gives what can be received in order to strengthen the finite intellect so that it can grow to receive Godself more and more. "As unto little ones I gave you milk and not meat, because you were not yet ready," St. Paul explained in 1 Cor 3:2, speaking on behalf of God. The divine names, along with the whole of the created world, are for Dionysius the way that God communicates himself to creatures who are still only able to take in creaturely milk and are not yet ready for divine meat.

So a divine name is a phenomenon in between the unknowable divine essence that remains forever hidden from us, and the material entities of the world through which God also communicates himself. This means that divine names are porous to the divine essence even as they are present in material entities. Dionysius had allegedly written a treatise attempting to explore the hidden divine essence titled *Theological Outlines* and another that explored how material creatures are divine communications titled *Symbolic Theology*. Unfortunately, both treatises are lost, leaving us with only *On the Divine Names*, which, as noted, lies between these two. Divine names, while inhabiting creaturely constitutions, are not themselves material. Nor are they identical with the divine essence. Rather, they are ways in which God speaks to us about himself so as to uplift us more and more into his unknowable essence.

NAMING GOD "BEAUTY"

By far the most important step in the Christian theology of beauty was taken when Dionysius named God "beauty." As

7. Aristotle, *On the Heavens*, bk. 1, ch. 6.

we have seen, the traditions that preceded him had been rather reluctant to take this step. No doubt, part of this reluctance stemmed from the fact that naming God beauty could potentially compromise the divine transcendence since there is such a "this worldly" dimension to beauty. Moreover, naming God beauty also ran the risk of engendering a theological pantheism, where any distinction between God and creatures is lost. Dionysius was more than in tune with such risks, and his decisive step was taken with the utmost care.

Along with naming God "beauty" Dionsyius had taken another step that would in part secure against either any compromise of divine transcendence or any kind of pantheism. Recall how Greek philosophers distinguished the originating principle, which they identified as the One, from the first emanation *nous*. It was a distinction without any unity, despite the fact that later generations of Neoplatonists would flirt with some kind of unity. If the One was truly one it could have no relations whatsoever. As the first emanation, *nous* was thought to turn back toward the One and so thought to have a relation to it. But it was only ever considered a one-way relation.

In his theological project, Dionysius saw in these two principles two aspects or facets of the one God: God in himself (corresponding to the One) and God in his act of creative communication (corresponding to *nous*). This meant, among other things, that Neoplatonic transcendence, which was conceived as absolute isolation from any relation whatsoever, was transformed into Christian transcendence, which was conceived as absolute relation to all things most intimately. In other words, for Dionysius, God's oneness was not an isolated oneness but rather a unique way of relating—absolute relation. It was one because God is the only one who is able to relate in this way.

Naming God "beauty" corresponded to this unity-in-plurality between God in himself and God in his creative communication. Recall that the beauty Dionysius inherited was not the modern sense of beauty as either something in the eye of the beholder or mere outward prettiness. Rather, it was the more deeply organic sense relating to call, existence, symmetry, simplicity, desire in itself, anagogy, the *paraprosdokian*, unity-in-plurality, and love.

When Dionysius appropriated the name beauty to God as God is in himself, he was not attempting to determine God's incomprehensible essence. Throughout his works, especially in his treatise *Mystical Theology*, Dionyius explains how there are two ways of approaching God. The first way is called positive, or *cataphatic*, theology. It is a mode of theology that approaches God through images, symbols, and concepts—in effect, by using positive means to think and speak about God and the mysteries of faith. They are positive because they *affirm* some sort of intelligible content within the finite limits of a concept, image, or idea. Because God exceeds any such images, thoughts, or concepts the human mind is able to construct or borrow from the world, this mode of theology falls short of communicating God, a feature that one must always bear in mind when applying it.

But the limitations that follow this first mode of theology can in many ways be overcome by the second mode, called negative, or *apophatic*, theology. This mode of theology works by intellectually negating every image, thought, or concept that is used to convey God. It is a mode of theology that aspires to always bear in mind the limitations in any positive act of thinking about God. By negating a given image, thought, or concept—as in "God is *not* this image"— the theological mind is elevated to a place beyond what was negated and there opened to allowing newer and different images, thoughts, and concepts to aid the theological task. Once those images are beheld, they too must be negated, and the ascent continues.

When Dionysius names God in himself "beauty," then, it is an act of naming that is primarily rooted in negative, or *apophatic*, theology. Drawing from both his biblical and Greek sources, Dionysius saw how God in himself was both the plenitude of all form (Exodus) and the infinite sea of beauty (Plato). The capacity to cause all forms was both a divine power and, as Neoplatonism had maintained, a power of beauty. But this is not to say anything directly positive about God. Rather, for Dionysius it is to say, with his sources, that God as fullness and giver of all form is *not without* beauty. In fact, if form is the foundation of beauty in things, and if God gives this, then it follows that the divine "being" must be the excess of all forms (and more, since even "excess of all forms" is categorical and so must be negated). The only way to properly speak or think this is to conceive God as none of the forms that can be encountered. God is the form of all forms and more. God is beyond form, which although appearing positive as expressed in words, is really negative in substance as the infinite substance that births every substance.

In this sense, naming God beauty identifies God as a transcendent plenitude of substance. As a name that identifies God in himself, beauty, just like God's very substance, is eternal, unchanging, available to all, and given to all beautiful things. Here is how Dionysius describes it:

> And God is called Beautiful as being at once beautiful and super-beautiful, and always being under the same conditions and in the same manner beautiful, and neither coming into being nor perishing, neither waxing nor waning; neither in this beautiful, nor in that ugly, nor at

one time beautiful, and at another not; nor in relation to one thing beautiful and in relation to another ugly, nor here, and not there, as being beautiful to some, and not beautiful to others; but as itself, in itself, with itself, one, always being beautiful, and as having beforehand in itself pre-eminently the fontal beauty of everything beautiful.[8]

Scholars have long recognized the similarity between this passage and a passage from Plato's *Symposium* (210e–211a), indicating the influence that Plato had on Dionysius. However, where Plato identified beauty as a principle, Dionysius appropriates it as a name for God, which enabled him, unlike Plato, to recognize the unity between beauty and the good in God.

For Dionysius, the primary name for God is the good which all things desire. But saying this leaves the matter somewhat abstract and indeterminate. Naming God beauty identifies the way in which the good begins to manifest itself more concretely in the form of things themselves. (It might be helpful to recall here how the names identify distinct, though not separate, dimensions of God; that is, they are unified in the Godhead himself, and so identify a similarity of substance, while identifying a distinction in terms of how that substance is known by us). Beauty in this sense is the good as the good comes closer to the desire of the human person, who is a creature of not only abstract, intellectual desire, but also of concrete, material desire. As the form of all form, that is, as the plenitude of all formal content, God is beauty both as an abstract center of all desire (the good) and as the concrete forms this desire takes as it calls to the intellect. In order to more clearly illuminate this, Dionysius also relates beauty to light.

8. Dionysius, *On the Divine Names*, ch. 4, section 7.

Light is another name that Dionysius appropriates to God, drawing again from both biblical and Greek thought as a foundation. In the order of names, light follows the good and precedes beauty, as the preconditions for the more concrete manifestations of beauty. There are two important dimensions of God that the name light conveys, which correspond also to beauty.

First, light is the very first form that the good assumes as it proceeds from God into the created order. Light identifies the conditions under which anything can be perceivable and hence desirable and knowable. In this sense, light opens the way for, and sustains the content of, beauty.

Second, light reveals most completely how something can be a plenitude of substance that, even though distributing itself endlessly, is never in itself diminished. In this way, light is a perfect unity-in-plurality. Dionysius offers the example of many lamps in a house. The light from each would be united as one "combined radiance" that would be indistinguishable from each other, yet each would derive from a distinct source.[9] This dynamic is then transferred to God himself: "For the divine light never leaves behind its own unique inwardness, but multiplied and going forth, as becomes its goodness, . . . remains firmly and solitarily centered within itself in its unmoved sameness, and raises according to their own capacity those who lawfully aspire to it and makes them one after the example of its own unifying oneness."[10] Here one can recognize the anagogical dynamic that Dionysius also attributes to divine light, as well as the way in which all this has the power to unify without compromising difference. Faithful to the unity-in-plurality dynamic, Dionysius time and again emphasizes the significance of the individual creature, as the phrase "according to

9. Dionysius, *On the Divine Names*, ch. 2, section 4.

10. Dionysius, *Celestial Hierarchy*, ch. 1, section 2.

their own capacity" in the above citation exemplifies. When he describes divine beauty, we find all of these dynamics present:

> But, the superessential Beautiful (God) is called Beauty, on account of the beauty communicated from itself to all beautiful things, in a manner appropriate to each, and as cause of the good harmony and brightness of all things which flashes like light to all the beautifying distributions of its fontal ray, and as calling all things to itself (whence also it is called Beauty), and as collecting in all to itself.[11]

Light becomes a helpful way to envision beauty's capacity to distribute itself without in any way diminishing its own beauty. Like a flame that could potentially ignite an endless number of fires, God's beauty is such that it gives itself ceaselessly to all beautiful things.

Since both the good as that which all things desire, and light as the conditions in which things may be perceivable, desirable, and hence knowable, are ways in which God's name beauty can be discerned, it follows that God is also the source of all intelligibility. Identifying God in himself as a plenitude of formal content means that God is also the ground upon which things are intelligible. We have already seen this dimension of beauty in the preceding chapters, but it is worth noting how Dionysius gives it a bit more detail. Divine beauty is bound up with divine goodness, which makes things desirable as something to be known. It is also bound up with divine light, which is the condition in which things can begin to appear. But again, beauty identifies the way in which light begins to take even more specific, concrete form through color, shape, magnitude, size, etc.

11. Dionysius, *On the Divine Names*, ch. 4, section 7.

The influence of both Augustine and Dionysius for the developing Christian theological tradition of beauty cannot be overstated. Thanks to their creative contribution, later generations of scholars would come to know the God at the heart of Christianity as a God who is beauty itself.

DISCUSSION QUESTIONS

1. What does it mean to say that Dionysius is an "unknown" monk? How might this "unknown" status contribute to his approach to divine beauty?

2. How does Augustine's approach to beauty and the identity of beauty with God compare with the Jewish, Greek, and Pauline traditions?

3. What might Dionysius contribute to how we "speak" about or to God?

4. How is Dionysius's approach to beauty a synthesis of both the Greek/Neoplatonic tradition and the Jewish tradition?

5. How do both Dionsyius and Augustine contribute to the notion of beauty as a name of God, and therefore to God's public identity?

4

BEAUTY AT THE DAWN OF THE MIDDLE AGES

IF THE ASSOCIATION BETWEEN beauty and the Middle Ages seems odd, it is only because we are clouded by the myth of the so-called "dark ages." As a name used to identify the period from anywhere between the sixth to the fourteenth century, "dark ages" is grossly misleading and no serious scholar today still uses such language. It is a term that derives from a particular ideology rather than anything historically accurate. What is "dark" depends entirely upon the values that one believes illuminate the darkness. Identifying the medieval world as "dark" was the result of a way of thinking that possessed the minds and hearts of those living in what they believed was an age of "Enlightenment." In this case, "Enlightenment" meant the triumph of one kind of rationality, mastery over the natural world, and a slow but efficient estrangement between faith and reason. The

"Enlightenment" became the dominating ideal for what many today call the project of modernity.

As these dimensions of modern thinking gained momentum, certain mythologies arose as exaggerated, if not entirely false, narratives intended to support modernity's *raison d'etre*. One of the most famous and still well-versed narratives, at least in the public realm, is that of the "dark ages." In light of this, then, it is worth asking: How could an age of such darkness have said so much about God's beauty? How could it have created something like the university system as a way to preserve past wisdom and to unify the various pursuits of human learning? Indeed, how could it have given us the awe-inspiring cathedrals we still continue to visit today?

As we will see in this chapter, the dawning of the Middle Ages was a time in which beauty was flourishing in a number of ways, but most especially within theological thought. Beauty's illumination of the mysteries of God and the world among scholars of this period serves to undermine the mythology of the so-called "dark ages."

THE MIDDLE AGES

Although scholars still debate precisely when the Middle Ages began, there seems to be enough of a consensus for the year 529.[1] This is the year that Emperor Justinian officially closed the Platonic Academy and in effect brought to an end the last great institution of the ancient world. The Roman Empire by this time had undergone a split between the East and the West. The Western part of the empire, since the time of Augustine, had begun to crumble from internal decadence, moral decay, and external invasion from a number of foreign tribes. In the Eastern part of the empire,

1. Cf. Pieper, *Scholasticism*, 15–25.

things were quite different. Around the year 330 Constantine—the first Roman emperor to not only convert to Christianity but to legislate social tolerance for Christianity in the Edict of Milan—had moved the capital to Byzantium, which became known as Constantinople in his honor. From that time on well up until the era of the Crusades in the thirteenth century, and the eventual fall of Constantinople in the mid fifteenth century, the region flourished politically, artistically, economically, and intellectually.

Amidst the crumbling Western part of the empire, steps had to be taken to preserve the treasures of the ancient world. A group of scholars, known as Encyclopedists, set themselves to the task of copying and preserving as much of the ancient wisdom as they could. Cassiadorus (480–575), Isadore of Seville (570–636), and the Venerable Bede (672–735), to name perhaps three of the most well known, understood the urgency of gathering as much material from the ancient world as possible. It was a task that consumed almost all of their time, which meant that they were limited in how they could add their own creative thought to the immense body of literature before them. Original theological and philosophical thought slowed down during this period, though only as a result of the constraints of time and the urgency of the task at hand. Nevertheless, a great deal of the theology of beauty was passed on through these important figures.

Handing on what they received from the classical tradition, these figures continued to view beauty as symmetry and simplicity, a proportion that enables a more original transcendent unity to emerge. Combined with the music theory that they encountered within Greek literature, beauty also became bound up with harmony and commensuration, but one that always pointed toward a more perfect, eternal harmony between the soul and God. At times, these

Encyclopedists stressed the association between beauty and light, which had already become common to late antiquity. Even though the works of Dionysius were unknown to them, much of what they emphasized about the relationship between the beauty in the world and God perpetuated its own unique way of understanding the association between beauty and the divine. Bede, for instance, held that the beauty of the natural world was itself a sign of divine grace,[2] while Cassiadorus believed that the harmony experienced in the world was a foretaste of eternal bliss.[3] Perhaps it was because theirs was a time of immense transition and upheaval that beauty announced itself with greater vigor or, perhaps, it was because they understood the important role that beauty performed in the overall approach to learning and thinking. In any case, the fact remains that these scholars were foundational for preserving the theological tradition of beauty.

JOHN SCOTUS ERIUGENA (815–77)

When it comes to a Christian theology of beauty, and the association between beauty and God, few figures during this time are as important as the Irish scholar John Scotus Eriugena. Not only was he one of the first to translate and comment upon the works of Dionysius, but his own major work—the *Periphyseon*, or *On the Divisions of Nature* (*De divisione naturae* is its Latin title)—made a significant impact on how the Dionysian divine names were understood. Eriugena's thinking was influenced primarily by Dionsyius, as well as Augustine, and some of the more important Eastern Fathers. Consequently, there was a strong Neoplatonic

2. Bede, *Ecclesial History of the English People*, bk. 1, ch. 7.
3. Cassiodorus, *On the Liberal Arts*, bk. 5.

flavor to his interpretation of Christianity, which made the theology of beauty in many ways central to his thinking.

Some might say that Eriugena went too far with the notion of beauty as a divine name in Dionysius. There are passages in his *Periphyseon* where he so closely identifies created beauty with divine beauty that he comes across as a pantheist. For example, in one of the most controversial sections, he writes "it follows that we ought not to understand God and the creature as two things distinct from one another, but as one and the same thing."[4] Taken in itself, this passage certainly seems to validate the charge of pantheism. And in fact, at the Council of Sens in 1225, many of the ideas in his book were condemned, though some scholars suggest Eriugena is only implicated by association since, at the time, there was a great deal of ambiguity surrounding the texts that bore his name.[5]

When one reads carefully the section in which the passage above appears, one finds that such exaggerations of the Creator/creature relationship are Eriugena's way of trying to overcome many of the divisions that he believed had become too exaggerated in the opposite way. Other passages seem to counter, or at least temper, the charge of pantheism, indicating instead that Eriugena was struggling to articulate the mystery of God's relationship to the world. For example, he claimed that all created things are both eternal and made at the same time; that is to say, creation is eternal insofar as it shares in God's eternal creative power, but it is made insofar as it comes about through the divine Word. In any case, Eriugena's belief about the relationship between God and creation derived from the influence of the Dionysian divine names theology and especially the name beauty.

4. Eriugena, *Periphyseon*, bk. 3, ch. 17.
5. See Moran, *Philosophy of John Scottus Eriugena*, 85–91.

For Eriugena, the beauty of creation not only bespeaks the beauty of God; it is the very presence of God Himself. Again, in his *Periphyseon* he writes, "God alone is the supreme and real goodness and beauty. For He Himself is whatever in creatures is understood (to be) really good and really beautiful and really lovable."[6] This does not mean that Eriugena believed God is somehow as knowable or comprehensible as things in the world. Rather, for him beauty was conceived above all as an inexpressible unity constituted by a harmony of all diverse components. The beauty in things is not in things insofar as they are taken in isolation from one another, but rather insofar as they are things in a community of relations intended by God. It is a community where one creature's beauty is not only a source of attraction to others, but also a power that provokes the desire to imitate the perceived beauty in new and unique ways. Consequently, things are only beautiful to the extent that they are visible within this community. In this context, the knowability or intelligibility of creatures, which is their beauty, is the divine voice calling the knowing intellect—through creatures—ever more into the divine unity-in-diversity.

The impact of Eriugena's theology of beauty cannot be overstated. Not only did it invest the created world with immense value, but also further solidified the union of beauty and human thought. In other words, where today we tend to associate beauty with something other than thought—an intuition, impulse, or spontaneous judgment perhaps (none of which are wrong, but rather taken in themselves, incomplete)—Eriugena, following Dionysius, found in beauty a power that provides the intellect a way to see things as they are in light of divine beauty. In this sense, reason was coming more and more into contact with the

6. Eriugena, *Periphyseon*, bk. 1, ch. 74.

way of orienting itself toward God that had always been at the heart of Christianity. Within Eriugena's inheritance of this Christian bequest, a new frontier was opening itself for theological exploration wherein reason could discover an intimacy with beauty.

ST. FRANCIS OF ASSISI (1181–1226)

Theology has always posed something of a risk to the Christian tradition. The Incarnation identified the act whereby the God—who is invisible, untouchable, indeed entirely transcendent of the material order as well as entirely immanent to it—enters into that very order so that, as St. Catherine of Sienna concluded, God could "come as close as possible to human beings." It was a closeness that marked a point of concrete encounter with a God who seemed otherwise distant in the way something abstract is. At its heart, theology is perhaps best identified with the eleventh-century figure Anselm of Canterbury's famous formulation "faith seeking understanding." But precisely here is where the risk arises: whenever understanding usurps the authority of faith and pushes its way into the center of the theological enterprise, the concreteness of the Incarnation risks being emptied of its most effective dynamic. Theology then begins a slow migration into the realm of abstract thought where it turns its focus away from its personal, concrete source in Jesus Christ and instead loses itself in its principles, concepts, and categories. So long as faith remains the authority, theology is capable of not only fostering profound understanding, but also safeguarding against this risk.

Toward the end of the twelfth century, in the figure of Francis of Assisi, beauty reminded the world of its capacity to take a person out of the abstract realm of the mind into the concrete realm of creatures. Remarking on the power of beauty in Francis's way to God, St. Bonaventure wrote "[i]n things of beauty, [Francis] contemplated the One who is supremely beautiful, and led by the footprints he found in creatures, he followed the Beloved everywhere."[7]

Francisco di Pietro di Bernardone was born to a wealthy family around the year 1181. His father was a silk merchant who employed Francis at an early age. According to a biography written by St. Bonaventure, Francis felt the stirrings of a deep and profound love of the poor very early on. Yet Francis's passionate spirit inspired him to travel to Apulia and enlist as a soldier in the service of a certain Count, which consequently led him to war in the year 1204. On his way there, however, it is said that he had a vision of the Lord who asked him, "who can do more for you, the Lord or the servant? The rich man or the poor?" Francis replied that a rich Lord could do more for him than a poor servant, to which the vision responded saying, "why then do you leave the Lord for the servant, the God of infinite riches for a poor mortal?" Francis replied by asking, "Lord what would you have me do?" "Return home," said the voice, "for the vision you have seen will bring to pass a spiritual work not by human counsel but by divine disposition."[8]

Francis returned home the following day and began to withdraw from worldly affairs. Obviously this meant leaving not only the family business, which raised the ire of his father, but also the life he previously had, a life with friends, festivities, and frolic. Some legends recount his departure from the worldly affairs as a tense struggle with his father. The more Francis became absorbed by his passion for the poor, suffering Christ, the more disinterested he became

7. Bonaventure, *Legenda Maior, IX, I: Fonti Francescane*, no. 1162, 911. Quoted in John Paul II, *Letter to Artists*, §19.

8. This event is recounted in St. Bonaventure, *Life of Saint Francis of Assisi*, 14.

in his family's wealth and prosperity. At one point with his father out of the country for travel, so it is alleged, Francis sold several of his father's fabrics and offered the money to a priest at a nearby church for restoration purposes. When the priest learned whose son Francis was, he refused the money, provoking Francis to throw it onto a ledge and leave it there. When his father returned, he became enraged to learn of this incident and immediately dragged Francis before the bishop. His father demanded that Francis renounce the inheritance he had coming, and in a dramatic gesture of consent, Francis stripped naked in the town square in front of hundreds of onlookers and laid his clothes at the foot of his bishop.

It is difficult to verify such accounts, though as of now there is no reason to think them false. What is notable about all this is the way in which Francis's way to God stemmed not only from a poverty or a giving up, but from an embrace of the divine abundance. Illuminated by the plenitude of divine Beauty, Francis could see that the only way in was to renounce one's attachment to anything of the world. But this was not a rejection of worldly things so much as it was an embrace of their full and true value.

Francis was not a theologian in the conventional, scholarly, sense, but his religious genius is beyond question. It was a genius that flowed through his love for the God who is Beauty itself. As we saw in chapter 2, one of the most significant attributes of beauty is that it must manifest itself in the particular. Seen from this perspective, the God who is beauty itself could not remain distant and aloof but rather, as beauty, "pitched his tent and dwelt among us," as John 1:14 puts it, becoming a particular person in a particular culture in the personhood of Jesus of Nazareth. It was through the person of Jesus that Francis came to love God's beauty and came to such an intimate union with Jesus that

Francis's very body would eventually bear the very wounds of Jesus when he received the stigmata.

Perhaps the single most important contribution to a theology of beauty that Francis made was a return to the particular individuality of Jesus. In the Incarnation, God had entered completely into the particularities of human life. It was an event that inspired the gathering of a community not only of practice but also of thoughtful reflection. Both became part of the life of the Church, even though as the tradition developed practices and reflection would become immensely diverse.

In part, this diversity derived from the revelation of the Word, the second person of the Trinity, in the person of Jesus Christ. As the Word, the Son bore the divine plenitude of being and form—that is to say, bore the divine Beauty itself—allowing those devoted to Christ the Word to find him anywhere. But it also shifted the focus from the particular person of Jesus Christ toward the universal, and hence abstract, dimension of truth available in the Word.

By the time Francis arrived on the scene, theological reflection in part had begun to center itself in the universal at the expense of particularities. The theological tradition had in many ways abstracted Christ from his particularity and made him into another Platonic ideal form. Although this may have been a necessary condition for theological reflection, Francis understood all too well that the Christian faith is nothing if not centered upon the concrete person of Jesus Christ—the man who lived, who walked the dirt of the earth, who wore sandals, ate and drank with his friends, laughed, wept, bled, suffered and died. Without ever intending to, Francis's devotion to Jesus the person led to something of an intellectual revolution, which as such instituted a new way of understanding God, beauty, and the world. Louis Dupré, explaining Francis's aesthetic, puts it as follows:

> [For Francis] God's incarnation in an individual human nature religiously legitimated the uninhibited representation of the physical features of Christ and of those whose lives had been touched by him. It also granted individual form a definitiveness which it had not possessed before. Thus began a daring cosmic symbolism that endowed each facet of nature with inexhaustible expressiveness . . . This symbolic naturalism gave birth to a new aesthetic. . .[9]

The primary feature of this new Franciscan aesthetic consisted in prioritizing the individual form over and against any universal reality that the form may be thought to communicate. No longer were particular things in the world merely openings to some greater universal form. Instead, it was the universal forms themselves that bore witness to the particular individual inasmuch as these universal forms were thought to intend that particular individual. This gave particular beings an ontological priority—a priority at the level of existence—over universal truths. Universal truths, especially those associated with the Word, may have an epistemic priority—priority at the level of knowledge—but for Francis, knowledge of Christ flowed from love for Christ first. This focus on the particularity of the concrete person of Jesus constituted something of a spiritual revolution in a time when the universal truths of faith were more and more laying claim to cognitive authority.

This led Francis to see God everywhere in the natural order. In his *Canticle of Brother Sun*, Francis expressed his belief that to love God one must love every one of God's works. Here, the Pauline union between the invisible things

9. Dupré, *Passage to Modernity*, 36.

of God and the visible things God has made finds its most intimate closeness. The elements of the earth (air, water, fire, etc.), the plants, the animals, and even bodily death are all praised as not only members of the family God has created ("Brother Sun," "Sister death" as he called them) but as ways to God. Nothing, however, leads to God with as much power as the God-man himself, and, as the first rule of his order testifies, it is the concrete person of Jesus Christ that occupies the center of Francis's way.

It was not an easy way, to be sure, and required a great deal of sacrifice from aspiring monks. But Francis's way was much more than a mere giving up. Every sacrifice was "for the sake of the Kingdom," which meant that sacrifice was always done in order to further allow oneself to be elevated more deeply into the abundance of the divine being itself. In renouncing the goods associated with this world, Francis envisioned a way of opening oneself to the plenitude of being identified as God's beauty. This renunciation could not be done in a spirit of fleeing the world, but in a deep and profound love for the particular beings that made the world what it was. And this could only be done by turning oneself to the particular person of Jesus Christ whose visible manifestation of God was broken in order to give the divine beauty more completely.

In terms of the developing theological tradition of beauty, the unintended consequences of Francis's spiritual revolution were a swinging of the pendulum, so to speak, back to the particular, the concrete, the here and now. As we saw early on in this tradition, beauty is "difficult" (as Plato had observed) because it so easily inhabits both the universal and the particular, the abstract and the concrete, the spiritual and the material. To the extent that the Latin West had fallen too far toward the universal, abstract, and spiritual aspects of beauty, Francis had initiated a return to the particular, the material, and the concrete. And it was a return that would become the mark of his legacy. It would also establish something of a crisis in the developing Christian tradition insofar as it foregrounded the dilemma that beauty had always posed: How are we to mediate material and spiritual beauty? How can we avoid tilting the necessary balance involved in this tension?

BEAUTY IN EARLY SCHOLASTICISM

Nowhere was this tension confronted with more vigor than in the schools of the early Middle Ages. The origins of the university system can be found in the monastic movement that emerged in the late ancient world. These monasteries, which served as medicinal, agricultural, and educational centers, flowered into various schools, which were identified either with a certain religious order or a particular patronage. At the heart of all such schools, however, was what might be considered a sacramental approach to existence: an approach that sees in every created thing an infinite spiritual depth. For these communities, beauty was an *event* that disclosed the way in which the material, observable order of the world opened to a more original and more powerful spiritual, invisible divine ordering. It is easy to see the various primary influences of incarnation, Paul's interpretation of the incarnation in Romans 1:20, Dionysius and Neoplatonism, Eriugena, and others in almost all of these various schools.

Differences among the schools arose in terms of emphasis. When examining the God-world relationship through the experience of beauty, which is normative? God is invisible, as Paul explained, though he can be "clearly seen" in the things he has created. Is it the case, then, that God, as purely spiritual beauty, is the standard or measure by which the beauty of creatures is discerned? Does this further mean that without at least a pre-apprehension of God's beauty it is not possible to truly apprehend beauty in the world? Or is it the case that the beauty of creatures contributes in an ever-expanding way to discerning the purely spiritual beauty of God? Since God is not some object alongside other objects, does it not follow that any apprehension of his beauty can only derive from an ever-expanding entry into the event of his beauty as given in the beauty of creatures? For us today, this may seem nothing more than a "chicken or egg" issue, but for the theologians of the twelfth and thirteenth century, it had profound theological implications. In many ways, the genius of these early scholastic thinkers derives from their unwillingness to acquiesce to the either/or assumed by the tension, but instead to dwell in that tension, opening themselves to the presence of Christ in whom that tension became a person. Rather than a hard and fast choice toward one side or the other, the figures who defined the various schools of the twelfth century can be thought of as emphasizing certain dimensions within that tension.

Among the various schools during the early Middle Ages, three stand out: the Cistercians, the Victorines, and the School of Chartres. In what is now a classic work on medieval aesthetics, Edgar de Bruyne describes the three primary schools and their particular approaches to beauty by using the image of the eye. The Cistercian approach saw beauty with a "spiritual eye," the Victorine approach with a "physical" eye, and the School of Chartres with the scholarly eye of the intellect.[10] This taxonomy will help us to better examine more closely each of these schools.

As de Bruyne's image suggests, the Cistercians, among whom some of the more notable include Bernard of

10. De Bruyne, Études d'esthétique medieval, 1:625–71.

Clairvaux, Thomas of Cîteaux, and Baldwin of Canterbury, emphasized the superiority of spiritual beauty, most often associated with the inner dimensions of human nature, over the physical beauty that is made visible in creatures. This gave rise to the peculiar tension that marked Cistercian thought: the physical beauty of creatures was considered both the opposite of spiritual beauty as well as its manifestation. How did they proceed to mediate these two dimensions? Following Dionysius and, through him, Plotinus, the Cistercians found in the phenomenon of light a way of dealing with this tension. They looked to the soul as the primary locus of beauty, and interpreted it according to principles of light. In the same way that light is both an act of illumination and a source of attraction, they applied these to the beauty of the soul: the soul's internal relationship with spirit revealed beauty as "claritas" (clarity, illumination); the soul's external relationship with the world revealed beauty as "caritas" (love, attraction). In this way, the tension within beauty's spiritual and physical forms is resolved in the moral life, that is, a life that concerned the relation between beauty and the good rather than any normative criteria of moral behavior.

The two dimensions of the beauty in the soul were both oriented toward the good. *Claritas* was oriented toward the good in an absolute way, as its desire is always for the good itself. *Caritas* was oriented toward the good in a relative way, seeking and displaying beauty in the good of worldly relationships (echoing Augustine). Spiritual beauty, although emphasized, was recognized as it descended into the world to make itself known in the way that light shows itself not only by glowing from an origin but also by illuminating other objects. As with Augustine, Cistercians believed that it did this only to gather and take the soul back into itself. This meant that the beauty of physical forms always carried a risk of luring the soul into themselves rather than anagogically elevating the soul into the true beauty of the spirit. Available to the soul in its movements, however, was the "hidden inspiration of grace"[11] that the Cistercians associated with beauty. Cast in a life of devotion, the soul could pursue beauty confident that this hidden inspiration would enable it to avoid the risks of physical beauty.

The School of St. Victor, or the Victorine School, was originally founded by William of Champeaux, and included some of the greatest figures of the Middle Ages such as Richard of St. Victor, Thomas Gallus, and perhaps the most well-known and influential, Hugh of St. Victor. As a school, it drew more deeply from Eriugena's theological synthesis and Dionysius's divine names approach to beauty than did the Cistercians. The emphasis for them fell on the worldly dimension of beauty, which is why de Bruyne describes them as seeing beauty with a "physical eye." They held that the beauty of created things is the very presence of absolute, divine beauty. This is not to say that they believed created beauty to be superior to divine beauty. For the Victorines, true beauty was indeed divine beauty, but precisely *as beauty* it gives form and shape to all things visible and intelligible. Hugh of St. Victor wrote "the most obvious image of God is the beauty of his creatures,"[12] capturing well how God's beauty shines through the beauty of what he has made. In this way, every creature is endowed in its very being with a nature that is efficaciously symbolic; that is to say, it is a symbol in a way that, more than representational, is event-inducing.

Thus, for the Victorines, the beauty of creatures was symbolic of divine beauty. As noted, this symbolism, more than referential, was event-inducing, generating a real and

11. Thomas of Cîteaux, *Commentary on the Song of Songs*, bk. 6, ch. 4.

12. Quoted in De Bruyne, Études III: 238.

potentially contemplative encounter with God. Beauty was configured as an anagogical power given to the intellect through creatures, making the world of creatures a book written by God. The capacity to read this book, of course, required that the intellect be properly disposed through scripture (God's other book) and a life of faith. In any event, it is not difficult to see how both Dionysius and Eriugena influenced this school even if the Victorines did not go as far as Eriugena.

As the soul is elevated through the beauty of the world, it comes to know its own beauty, which increases its capacity to receive and ascend into the spiritual beauty of God. As it more and more contemplates divine beauty given in the world, a sense of dissatisfaction is aroused in the soul, which, through contemplation, becomes more and more aware of the inadequacy of created forms. Here we can see where the Victorine school reflects a similarity with the Cistercians. But where the Cistercians react to this dissatisfaction with a certain moral resistance, for the Victorines the dissatisfaction is more akin to Dionysian unknowing, where the excess of divine plenitude reveals itself in the failure of created beauty. Growing dissatisfaction with worldly beauty was a sure sign of an ascending soul.

It would not be inaccurate to locate the school of Chartres in between the Cistercians and the Victorines. Viewing beauty through the "eye of the intellect" meant an engagement with the physical beauty of the world, but an engagement that brought that encounter into the spiritual life of the intellect. Situated here in this between, it ought to come as no surprise that the Chartreans emphasized the symmetry and proportionality of beauty. In so doing, their focus was more on the natural world than God, since any proportionality presupposes limited terms. The Chartreans drew heavily from Platonic thought, and in particular

Plato's origin narrative *Timeaus* from which they developed the view that the nature of the world is most fundamentally mathematical, founded as it is upon a principle of proportionality. Just as an artist puts her unique presence into every work of art, so too it is by virtue of the divine presence in the world that its beauty appears through proportion. This is why mathematics was so important for the Chartrians. It was a language of nature that enabled them to peel back the transience of the world and perceive its eternal structure. Hence, the beauty revealed by mathematics, which grounded all proportionality, signified the presence of the eternal in the world and therefore signaled the world's highest beauty. In this sense, the natural world was seen as the self-offer of the divine to satisfy the desires of intellectual inquiry. Hans Urs von Balthasar has observed what he called the "universal teaching of Chartres": because God informs everything by giving it being, God is said to be every being with respect to the given form.[13] This may sound pantheistic, confusing creation with God. However, for the Chartrians God is pure form itself, which means that as such God transcends all created forms as the only form that is pure form. God gives himself in "bite size pieces," so to speak, or as St. Paul says, as "milk" rather than "meat" (cf. 1 Cor 3:2), to the searching intellect. But God is always greater, as Anselm and Augustine had made clear. In the School of Chartres, then, one finds that the beauty of the world is identified as the very presence of God, the eternal that is perpetually discovered through intelligible proportions of created entities.

The tensions that emerged with greater vigor within these influential schools of early scholasticism were in fact tensions that inhabited Christian thought from the

13. Balthasar, *Glory of the Lord*, 4:365. Augustine and Eriugena had also made similar claims.

beginning and continue to do so today. The unique approach to, and mediation within, these tensions is where the thrust of the schools' original contribution can be located. The questions that were raised by these early scholastics were much more than theological speculation, but were rather questions that sought to integrate Christian thought with Christian practice. The limits of language and concepts imposed by the "difficulty" of beauty—first recognized so long ago by Plato but remaining throughout the tradition of beauty—had the effect of pushing thought more deeply into beauty itself where things opened to their spiritual depth. Theirs was a sacramental, and at times liturgical, theological approach that aspired to understand how the world and everything in it could be viewed as a way to God. This approach, centered in divine beauty, left a lasting mark on scholastic posterity.

DISCUSSION QUESTIONS

1. How does the early medieval account of beauty provide substance for rethinking the notion of the "dark ages"?

2. What are some of the theological risks and benefits within John Scotus Eriugena's approach to beauty?

3. How does St. Francis's approach to God's beauty impact the way that you view both God and beauty?

4. How does St. Francis's theology of beauty serve theological discourse in general?

5. What were the unique attributes of the various schools in early medieval scholasticism with respect to how each contributed to identifying God with beauty?

6. How does the early medieval theology of beauty change your views of the Middle Ages in general?

5

THE MEDIEVAL THEOLOGY OF BEAUTY

As THE LAST CHAPTER began to argue, the medieval world, contrary to the mythology that misrepresents it today, was a world imbued with beauty. This chapter continues that argument by looking more closely at how the intimacy between reason and beauty, which began to take shape in Eriugena, Francis and others, culminates in the work of the thirteenth century, a time often referred to as the "High Middle Ages." As common experience often attests, sometimes the most profound beauty hides itself behind the seemingly ordinary, mundane, or even what may at first appear to be quite unattractive. Divine Beauty, as theologians have maintained, enters the world most fully as an infant to a poor, young woman and a common carpenter rather than adorned royalty. It is only to those with eyes willing to see it that such a profound beauty eventually reveals itself.

For many, the beauty of scholastic thought is equally difficult to see, hiding as it does behind texts that, as the philosopher G. W. F. Hegel described them, are "as prolix as they are paltry, terribly written and voluminous."[1] We have no need to deny that scholastic treatises lacked the decorated prose of many gifted writers of later generations. The schoolmen were far more interested in communicating divine things in an intelligible way than dressing it up for mass appeal. Some of the scholastics reached divine heights so dizzying that their attempt to communicate what they saw seemed to affirm Anselm's claim that indeed God is "that than which nothing greater can be thought." This chapter examines three of the most well-known and influential figures of the High Middle Ages: St. Albert the Great, St. Thomas Aquinas, and St. Bonaventure. The work of these figures testifies not only to the brilliance of the age, but to the power that reason finds when wedded to beauty.

ST. ALBERT THE GREAT (1193–1280)

Albert's theology of beauty is complex and is captured well in his treatises where he treats beauty, primarily his *Commentary on the Divine Names* of Dionysius, as well as his *On Beauty and Goodness*. This complexity can be summarized in the following way: for Albert, beauty is the good as it is known and loved in all its truth. On the surface this may not appear complex, but the primary terms that constitute it—beauty, good, truth, know, and love—identified phenomena that themselves were far more complex than they often appear to be. Before we examine this formula in more detail, it will be helpful to establish Albert's primary principle: form.

---

1. Hegel, *Complete Works* (*Sämtliche Werke*), 149.

The Form of Knowledge and Desire

The central principle that guided Albert's theology of beauty, and that allowed him to arrive at the above formula, was the concept of "form." A common medieval doctrine held that everything that is not God is composed of two or more principles. Only God is so simple as to be constituted by nothing but his own divine being. The divine being, so it was believed, was an infinite plenitude of all that was, is, and will be, but in a simplicity. That is, in itself it is not composed of these created entities even though it does give existence to them. Since only God is identifiable in this way, everything other to God must be in some way complex, that is, constituted by two or more "parts."

The most basic way that the constitution of creatures in the natural world was understood was to identify their two most fundamental principles. The first identifies the way in which all creatures in the physical world not only occupy the three dimensions of space, but also by which creatures move and undergo change, and this was called "matter." Matter is quite literally nothing without the second most fundamental principle "form." In simplest terms, form is that by which matter appears in just this way, just this shape, this color, this size, etc. Because form is what differentiates matter as "this" matter, it is also a principle of knowledge, or "that by which a thing is known."

Albert structured his theology of beauty around this principle of form, not at the expense of matter but as that by which all material phenomena are known and loved. It was commonly held that the divine being is unique in virtue of the fact that God alone is pure form, form itself free of any matter whatsoever. We have already seen how the phenomenon of light provided the Cistercians with a way of conceiving a surplus of substance that endlessly gives itself without diminishment. Although not as explicitly, light as a theological principle informed Albert's thinking as well. If we think about how a source of light like a lit match can, *in theory* at least, extend its light infinitely without diminishment—insofar as one match can ignite another, which can in turn ignite another, and so on—we can apply this to Albert's concept of form to better understand his approach to beauty.

God as pure form gives form to all things in his act of creation. Divine giving, unlike any other mode of giving that we might be familiar with, is not an extrinsic exchange, that is to say, not an event in time where some good is passed from God to creature. Nor is it a mode of giving by which the one who gives must be dispossessed of the given in order for the given to be received. Rather, divine giving happens at a level much deeper within a creature's very being. As Albert understood this, it meant that the divine giving of forms had both an intrinsic and an extrinsic dimension.

Although the position was not without debate in the Middle Ages, it was widely believed that God created not only form but also the matter that receives the form. Albert's theory maintained that God creates matter but only as a potency for the form that God eventually imbues into it. That is to say, matter in its original state—what the scholastics referred to as prime matter—is itself pure potency waiting to be called forth by the form it desires.

It is impossible for the human mind to positively conceive prime matter since concepts require actual substance, that is, something that exists. Even saying that it "desires" form is stretching terms. Prime matter can only be conceived negatively by identifying it as "that which is completely without form," which means it is nothing in itself. Albert maintained that it remains in a state of non-being until it is infused by the divine *kalon* (call), or divine beauty. As coming from a state of transcendence, God's divine call gives form extrinsically, that is to say, from beyond the creature's being. However, as a response is enabled by matter's potency for form there is also a sense in which the form emerges from within, arising intrinsically as the creature is more and more elevated into this divine call.

In the created order, the union of matter and form identifies the basis of existence. Existence, so it was believed by most of the scholastics, is the first perfection because it is the first way in which a creature shares in the good itself, shares in God's very being. Perfection did not mean "beyond mistakes" but rather the degree to which a thing was made, the finality of its being vis-à-vis its own unique form. Since all form derives from the divine plenitude of form, form is itself a communication of the good. For this reason, in Albert's theological thought, the good was prior even to existence as the first and most primordial of God's attributes. It was also, therefore, the first phenomenon given and shared by creatures, through which emerges their existence as unique beings.

Beauty Is the Good Known and Loved in All Its Truth

If we are to understand beauty as Albert did, it is necessary to view it in relation to both the good and the true. Albert followed the traditional idea, first coined by the Greeks but transformed into Christian currency, that the good is "that which all things desire." This is itself a far more complicated claim than at first appears. Today, it may strike us as an assertion about the subjective character of the good; whatever a person desires must therefore be good. Although not entirely wrong, this claim is incomplete. For Albert, desire is first provoked, or called forth, by the source of all good things, who is God. To say that God is the source of all good does not mean that God conforms himself to some idea of goodness outside himself. Rather, God quite simply is the good itself. Nor is God's goodness in competition with other goods. Rather, it distills itself into the many goods of the world. God's goodness is infinite goodness and so in the same way that mathematical infinity manifests itself in discrete numerical entities, so too does God's infinite goodness reveal itself in the multitude of goods in the world.

The goods of the world are, in part, God's way of attracting us to himself as the source of these goods. Whether material goods like food, shelter, clothing, etc., or immaterial goods like friendship, knowledge, or faith, every good that is given intends not only to satisfy a current desire but also to open the person's capacity for desire so that she may continue to ascend ever higher into the divine goodness itself. In this ascent, the person assimilates these goods to her very being and so, through these goods, nourishes herself on the divine good that gives them.

It is through desire that the human person becomes one with being by orienting herself to the good. The moral question concerning how human beings can assimilate themselves to things that only *appear* good, or to things whose good comes with a great deal of evil, is not necessary to consider here. Let us simply note that desire is perhaps the most powerful faculty that human beings possess. It can lead us toward the God who is the absolute good we seek, or it can imprison us in some particular, and so limited, good. It can delight us beyond measure or destroy us in ways unforeseeable. Whatever the case may be, desire is the first movement of the soul toward the otherness of being, and eventually toward the absolute otherness of God. Through desire, God calls us into union with Himself, which involves a union with what God gives in being.

The eventual assimilation between the human soul and the goods within being was identified by the scholars of the Middle Ages as "truth." The word that they most often used was "adaequation": truth is the *adaequation* between the mind and being, or the eventual harmony between intellect and existence. To put this in simpler terms, truth identifies the eventual union between the human intellect and what is, what exists, or what is real—and what is, or what is "real," is not some objectively, blue-printed fact, but that which is discernible only through participation in it. It is eventual because it follows a course that begins in desire. In this way, we can see how truth and existence are the same in substance, that is to say, the same in terms of *what* they are. However, they differ only in terms of *how* they relate to us. Truth is existence that is made conceivable, or knowable to the human intellect in a way that is clear and coherent.

As Albert understood so well, truth begins with desire for the good. In his treatise *On Beauty and Goodness*, Albert compares the relationship of desire to the good and the true in the way that medicine relates to nature; desire first exists as a fuller momentum toward the good before it is focused as truth in the same way that the fuller power of nature precedes the more specified power of medicine.[2]

So where does beauty come into all this? If we take a step back and review what we have considered so far, beauty's role will become clearer. All things desire the good and in so doing desire an end of some kind. In its original eruption, this desire is unformed, or unfocused, since it is at first oriented toward the infinite good that is God. In itself, the infinite divine good is an end that is never attained in this life. Rather than causing despair, this unattainable good is what continues to drive desire beyond the goods through which the divine good gives itself. When these

2. Albert the Great, *De Pulchro et Bono*, question 1, article 1.

goods are eventually acquired, they are assimilated to the intellect in the form of truth. At this stage, truth identifies the way in which the good, or being itself, has conformed to the requirements of human knowing (concepts, categories, symbols, etc.). As truth, then, the good that is desired is rendered more and more understandable even as it is pushed further into its infinite fullness. Albert envisions a process whereby the infinite good provokes desire, which leads to the eventual assimilation of the goods—through which the infinite good gives itself—in the form of truth.

The good and the true, then, identify two dimensions of the union of knowledge. The good is the end that is always being sought and that drives desire toward the variety of goods in the world, while the true is the conformity between what is desired and the human intellect, affirming the good as good by rendering it understandable. But what happens in between? Is it simply a two-step process where unformed, or unfocused, desire is simply transformed into truth? Or rather, is the process much more complicated?

As noted already, God is the form of all form, or pure form itself. As the infinite good, God's form draws all desire toward itself. But in order to do this, the divine form must condescend in such a way that it eventually conforms itself to the limits of the human intellect (as truth). The good does this in the mode of beauty giving rise to Albert's formula, "beauty is the good as it is known and loved in all its truth."

Another way that Albert identified beauty, which will provide clarity here, was to say that "beauty identifies a gathering power that shines beyond the parts it gathers." In other words, between the good in itself and the eventual adaequation of the good as truth, there is a mode by which the good gathers. The verb "gather" is, admittedly, somewhat vague—what exactly is gathered? For Albert, the gathering is both a generative act and an act of retrieval. As the good disperses itself into a variety of goods, there is a bond that remains between these various goods and the divine good itself. This bond is a gathering power and is beauty's first manifestation generating not only the unique properties of a particular good, but also allowing that particular good to attract desire beyond itself toward the infinite good.

This further means that every particular good is itself endowed with this gathering power. A thing's beauty, Albert maintained, is the unity of its form that shines over the various parts of that particular thing. When we perceive a thing's beauty, we perceive its transcendent form that gathers its distinct parts into its unity. Somehow, we perceive this unity precisely as it shines over the diversity of its parts but always and only through the diversity of its parts.

To make this more concrete consider the beauty of a piece of music. We can rightly say that this piece of music, or song, is beautiful, but when we stop to think about such a statement, what exactly do we mean by "this piece of music"? No one ever hears the whole piece in its entirety simultaneously, that is, as a unity. Rather, one only ever hears the song as it is communicated through the diverse sounds that constitute it over an equally diverse continuum of moments. Yet, somehow, we perceive the song as beautiful in itself. The song, then, is a helpful way to imagine the form that shines over the parts that constitute it. As a transcendent form, the song itself must communicate its beauty in time and space, which means through its constituent parts (notes, key, time signature, rhythm, etc.).

One of the most important points to take away from this is that for Albert, beauty is the gathering power that enables the good to begin to assume a more concrete form. Although beauty manifests itself in the degree of proportionality of that beautiful thing's parts, it is much less an attribute of the thing itself and much more a power, or event, whereby the infinite good that is always being sought assumes a perceptible form. In this sense, it is understandable why Albert would agree with Augustine's claim that the Son is the most beautiful of all since through the event of the Son's being sent, the infinite divine beauty becomes perceivable as a person. Perceptibility, as visibility opening to intelligibility in the context of the good as form, and in the context of truth as the eventual crystallization of that form in the intellect, became an enduring principle of Albert's theology of beauty, and perhaps no student of his was as important for bearing that legacy as Thomas Aquinas.

ST. THOMAS AQUINAS (1225–74)

Thomas was Albert's student and so took many of his cues from him. However, Thomas's greatness as a theologian in large part consisted in his capacity to synthesize a variety of sources into his theological vision. So although Albert may have been something of a guide for Thomas, Thomas was also influenced by Augustine, Dionysius, Anselm, Plato, Aristotle, and many of the early schools (not to mention Muslim and Jewish thinkers!). Like Albert, Thomas had written a commentary on Dionysius's *On the Divine Names*, in which he presents a prototype of the theology of beauty that appeared later in his *Summa Theologiae*. These prototypical remarks are important not only for how they demonstrate Thomas's knowledge of Dionysius, but also for how they develop and go beyond much of what Albert had said.

The most important idea that is found in his *Commentary on the Divine Names* is expressed as follows: "For the beauty of the creature is nothing other than the similitude of divine beauty participated in things."[3] Note that Aquinas

3. Thomas Aquinas, *Commentary on the Divine Names*, ch. 4, lecture 5.

says it is a *similitude* of divine beauty rather than a direct manifestation of divine beauty itself. A similitude is best understood as content that derives from a given source, and so has a unity or identity in that source, while at the same time bearing a significant difference from that source. Here we can begin to see how, early on, Thomas was in many ways very much in between many of the primary positions on beauty we have already seen.

Thomas followed many of the primary attributes of beauty handed on to him: beauty as a unity-in-plurality, beauty as an anagogical power, beauty as simplicity, beauty as a principle of determination, and beauty as form. As the reference above indicates, he saw beauty as itself a divine name, but gave a unique interpretation of what that meant. Although there is some controversy regarding how closely aligned he was with an authentic Dionysian position on this issue, it is clear that he followed Dionysius for the most part.

We have already seen how for Albert, beauty is a middle between the good and the true. Aquinas not only followed this idea, but gave it more explicit precision. Expressing this precision, Thomas wrote, "although beauty and the good are the same in substance . . . they differ in intelligible content: for beyond the good, the beautiful adds an order to the cognitive power that the good is of such a kind."[4] In other words, beauty is that attribute of being that allows the good to become more perceptible, or recognizable, since it allows for the good to be recognized in more limited ways while maintaining the bond that those limited goods have with their source. Without beauty, then, the good remains forever distant as an infinite end or goal that resides forever beyond human powers of perception.

In his celebrated *Summa Theologica*, Thomas presented a more developed account of beauty. Although there

4. Thomas Aquinas, *On the Divine Names*, ch. 4, lecture 5.

are a number of remarks about beauty throughout this enormous work, it is possible to highlight the two most important passages.

The first is found early on and occurs in a question wherein Thomas considers the relationship between the good and a final cause. In his reply to an objection that argued goodness and beauty are the same, and that therefore the good is a formal rather than final cause, Thomas distinguishes beauty from the good. He writes, "[t]he beautiful, however, bears upon a knowing power: for things are called beautiful which please when seen."[5] The word "seen" (*visa*) means more than the physical act of sight but includes the way in which all knowing is a kind of seeing. This is clear not only from the fact that "beauty bears upon a knowing power" but from the whole context of the reply itself, which distinguishes beauty from the good precisely because beauty, unlike the good, is the power that allows being to "assimilate" itself to the intellect in the form of knowledge. A thing can only be pleasing to sight when it is given in a proportion to the human capacity to perceive it. This is why, as Thomas concludes, beauty properly belongs to the intelligible content of a formal cause, that is to say, it belongs to the way in which human beings know a thing's form and so are themselves in-formed by that thing.

The second most well-known passage in Thomas's *Summa Theologica* where he discusses beauty is also his most theological. It is found in that section of the *Summa* that examines the Trinity.[6] In his response Thomas gives the "necessary conditions" for beauty both to manifest itself (from the side of beauty) and to become perceivable (from the side of the percipient). It was common for scholars of the Middle Ages to identify conditions that, rather than

5. Thomas Aquinas, *Summa Theologica* I, q. 5, a. 4, obj. 1.

6. Thomas Aquinas, *Summa Theologica* I, q. 39, a. 8.

being merely sufficient, were the *sine qua non* of the phenomenon in question. To be sure, however, Thomas will be misunderstood if he is read as providing a kind of litmus test, or blue print, for what is and is not beautiful. Necessary conditions were not preset blue prints, but rather emerged with the entity itself.

The text in question examines whether the "Holy Doctors"—by which Aquinas means Augustine, Hilary of Poitiers, and the authors of Scripture—fittingly appropriated certain attributes to the three persons of the Trinity. In the second book of his treatise *On the Trinity*, Hilary of Poitiers had attributed "eternity" to the Father, "beauty" to the Son, and "enjoyment of use" to the Holy Spirit. Thomas's account of beauty occurs when he affirms in what ways beauty is fittingly attributed to the Son. His response includes the following well-known statement:

> For with regard to beauty, there are three necessary conditions: first, certainly, wholeness or completeness (*integritas*), for some things which are impaired are ugly because of this; second, due proportion or harmony (*consonantia*); and third, clarity (*claritas*) from which some things have a bright color, and thus are said to be beautiful.

As Thomas proceeds to examine each of these three necessary conditions in more detail, his explanation concerns how these conditions correspond to the Son's relation to the Father. What this means is that, for Thomas, the Son quite simply is the first and most complete instance of beauty (a common scholastic idea by his time). To put it another way, there is no beauty outside the Son that can be used to evaluate the Son's beauty. The Son himself reveals the true nature of beauty so that, by him, beauty may become more illuminated and evident in the world.

As Thomas states, the first necessary condition is *integritas*: completeness or wholeness. Completeness, or wholeness, is fittingly attributed to the Son in terms of the Son's relation to the *nature* of the Father. More specifically, completeness, or wholeness, has a likeness to the property of the Son insofar as the Son has in himself the true and perfect nature of the Father. That is to say, the Son reveals what true completeness, or wholeness, looks like (so to speak) by truly and perfectly being the nature of the Father. Here we can see how, for Thomas, true and perfect completeness does not entail identity without difference. Rather, it is a unity-in-difference: the Son's completeness and wholeness in terms of the nature of the Father indicates both how the Son is unified with the nature of the Father, but in a unity that manifests itself in the Son's difference. In the Son, the true and perfect nature of the Father is made manifest without being identical to the Father and without exhausting everything about the Father. This means that the fullness of the Father is communicated in the particularity of the Son without in any way denigrating that fullness itself. The Son reveals that a true and perfect showing is both a unity and a distinction.

So what does this mean for beauty? In the Son's wholeness, or completeness, the first necessary condition for beauty is made known: beauty is the appearance of a thing's completeness or wholeness as it appears in the limited mode of its presence. It is an appearance that communicates fully and completely a thing's nature without being identical with, or exhaustive of, that thing's nature. To put it in plain terms, an encounter with beauty is an encounter with a thing's fullness as that fullness is communicated in the here and now. All things come from God's beauty, which is a fullness of intelligible content, and all things share in that fullness in their own unique way. Their beauty is their communication of this unique share in the divine fullness. This is a fullness that can only appear in time and space through that thing's unique form as a particular "this."

The second necessary condition is *consonantia*: due harmony or proportion. This agrees with the property of the Son in terms of the Son's relation as express *image* of the Father. As Thomas explains, a thing is said to be beautiful when it perfectly represents its archetype. As already implied in the first necessary condition, an image as perfect representation is both a unity and a distinction. As perfect, the image must share the nature of the archetype it images. But insofar as it is an image, it must be distinct from its archetype. As Thomas explained elsewhere, an image is never a perfect *likeness* but always bears a distinction from that which it images.[7] The Son is the perfect image of the Father because he expresses the wholeness or completeness of the Father's nature while also bearing his own distinction as the Son. This means that the Son is also the archetype of all images, which is to say there is no example of image outside the Son that can be brought in to explain or measure the quality of the Son as image. Rather, the Son is the measure of the quality of all other images.

So what does this mean for beauty? This particular necessary condition provides the required bond between a thing's wholeness (*integritas*) and the archetype that is manifest in that wholeness. Given the first necessary condition, it follows that there is a harmony or due proportion between the wholeness of the beautiful particularity and that which it images in its beauty. The wholeness of the beautiful particularity identifies the fullness of a thing's being in a way that can be communicated within the limits of time and space. This also means that the limits within time and space of that particular thing maintains a relationship

7. Thomas Aquinas, *Summa Theologica* I, q. 35, a. 2. ad. 1.

of due proportion or harmony with that fullness. All encounters with beauty, then, involve encountering this harmony or due proportion between the wholeness that is made visible and a fullness that shines precisely in and as a thing's beauty.

The third necessary condition, *claritas*, identifies the fullness as such. As Thomas explains, *claritas* agrees with the property of the Son insofar as the Son is the *Word* of the Father. As the Father's Word, the Son is the very source of all God's communicability and expressivity. As it is in the mind, a word is "representative of everything that is understood."[8] Although in the human mind, many words are necessary to represent all that is understood, in God "His one and only Word is expressive not only of the Father, but of all creatures."[9] In this respect, the Son is between the unknowable essence of the Father as his fullest expression, and the knowable content of creaturely forms as their cause.

So what does this mean for beauty? An encounter with a beautiful thing is an encounter with that thing's clarity, which is its fullness of form, or a fullness of its intelligible content. Thus the perception of a thing's beauty involves an encounter that provokes an intellectual union of knower with this fullness of intelligible content where knowledge not only begins but is also sustained. The beauty of the object being perceived, then, illuminates the one perceiving and in so doing elevates her intellect more profoundly into the beautiful thing's intelligible content. It is in this fullness of intelligible content where the beautiful object's power to generate images of itself resides, that is, its causal power. This third necessary condition, then, accounts for the way in which beauty bears an intellectual component both with respect to contemplation and with respect to making.

8. Thomas Aquinas, *Summa Theologica* I, q. 34, a. 3.
9. Ibid.

All three conditions are necessary because all three conditions "circumincess"—or continually and actively interpenetrate—one another. The Son is the perfect wholeness of the Father and so communicates, through the due proportion or harmony embodied in the particularity of the human nature assumed, the Son's clarity, or fullness of intelligible content, which is the Son's bond with the Father. In this, the Son reveals what are necessary conditions for beauty: an encounter with beauty is an encounter with a thing's wholeness or perfection (*integritas*) that communicates, through due proportion or harmony (*consonantia*), that beautiful thing's clarity, or fullness of intelligible content (*claritas*). As with the notion of "pleasing" we examined above, it is not the case that these three necessary conditions serve as a checklist or litmus test for determining what is and is not beautiful. Rather, these necessary conditions help to dispose a person toward beauty, that is, help to provide a person with a greater capacity to see the beauty of all things and therefore to be pleased by them.

ST. BONAVENTURE (1221–74)

Perhaps the greatest of the Franciscans, Giovani di Fidanza, known by his fellow Franciscans as Bonaventure, elaborated a theology that was everywhere informed by the same beauty that inspired St. Francis himself. The primary feature of Bonaventure's contribution to a theology of beauty concerns his focus. With few exceptions, there was among the scholastics of the thirteenth century a common approach to beauty and issues surrounding beauty. Naturally, Bonaventure was part of this community and so followed this approach. However, what distinguished his work was the fact that, more than most others, he devoted ample space to exploring these issues in detail. His theology of beauty bore the fingerprints primarily of Francis but read through the lenses of Dionysius, Augustine, Eriugena, and Anselm, as well as the Chartrians, Cistercians, and Victorines. The result of his exploration was a combination of many of the ideas that had preceded him but all of which were oriented within the context of his unique Franciscan approach to theology.

There is probably no clearer indication of the intimacy between reason and beauty in Bonaventure than in the first question of the Prologue to his *Commentary on the Sentences* of Peter Lombard. There, he describes the nature of theology in a way that resonates with principles from the tradition of beauty. He describes the object of theology as the "credible," which is to say the fullness of all that is worthy of the submission of our will and intellect. Insofar as it is a fullness, it exceeds our capacity for knowing it through our normal modes of cognition. Thus, the task of theology is somehow to make this "credible" more intelligible through the addition of reason. The "credible," as an excess of all intelligible content, is given in and as faith. Reason may be brought into this, but it does so only through the power given in love, which alone allows reason to cling to faith. This is why beauty was central to Bonaventure as that force beyond and within creation that not only provokes but also sustains the love that is the bond between reason and faith.

Bonaventure was an heir to many of the treasures handed on from the tradition of beauty, which he used to constitute his theological foundation. The soul of its nature desires God who is the infinite good. The faith that God gives draws the soul towards God more and more, giving anagogy a central place in Bonaventure's thought. One of his more famous treatises, the *Itinerarium Mentis in Deum*, or *The Journey of the Soul into God*, taught how human beings ascend to God through the things of the world, echoing the Pauline proclamation in Romans 1:20. From this perspective, creatures were understood as a way in which God speaks, a kind of language that made the whole universe a book in which God's presence can be discerned in every word.[10] Bonaventure held that not only could God be contemplated through things in the world, but that God was *in* them by essence, power, and presence. Bonaventure credits the "harmony of our created condition" for enabling the universe to serve as a ladder by which we can ascend through it to God. Here, a primary principle of beauty serves as both a constitutive property of things and an anagogical power.

In his theological synthesis of the many principles of beauty in the theological tradition, Bonaventure held that the beauty of the world served as the world's way of proclaiming God's power, wisdom, and goodness. He also held that the fullness of things in terms of their formal substance shared in this proclamation. But Bonaventure, as with his contemporaries, understood beauty to be a multifaceted phenomenon. The beauty of the world proclaimed the divine because the divine beauty itself manifests its illumination through these things.

This is not to say that all modes of beauty are equal. In his *Breviloquium*, Bonaventure observed a hierarchy of beauty: the beauty of the world is a lesser manifestation than the beauty of the church, which is itself a lesser manifestation of the beauty of the heavenly Jerusalem. But all tiers participate in the one, divine beauty that brings them into, and sustains, their existence. For this reason, there is the primacy of harmony in Bonaventure's account of beauty since beauty as a power requires the harmony between its

10. St. Bonaventure, *Journey of the Soul into God* (*Itinerarium Mentis in Deum*), ch. 2.

various modalities. In his *Commentary on the Hexaemeron*, he went so far as to say that "[t]here is no beauty except where there is a harmony of what is perceived with the one perceiving."[11] In this sense, beauty is above all an event whereby what is given not only calls to the recipient, but conforms itself to the faculties so as to allow for a fitting reception. In short, beauty is the event of union and ascent of the soul in its journey into God.

Ultimately, what distinguishes Bonaventure's contribution to the theological tradition of beauty is the fact that not only did he sharpen the focus of a scholastic vision that had been slightly broader among others, he applied this focus in an overarching spiritual ascent. At stake for him was not a contemplative, or reflective, account of the beautiful as an object of speculative inquiry. Rather, what was at stake was how beauty bears us on its wings into the life of the Crucified one, in whom all beauty has been revealed. What might be called his "applied theology of beauty" derived from Bonaventure's love and devotion to Francis's way to Christ. It was a way that emphasized the concrete particularity of the person of Jesus over any abstract systems of thought. Love was more of a priority for Bonaventure than even a sharpened intellect, although it might be said that love in his view serves to sharpen the intellect. But a sharpened intellect was not so much a priority as the will's capacity to cling to the God-man who empties himself to the point of sacrificing his very life in order that we might enter more and more into intimate union with him.

DISCUSSION QUESTIONS

1. How does Albert the Great's understanding of 'form' bring together other primary elements of beauty in

11. St. Bonaventure, *In Hexaemeron*, col. 14, 4.

earlier traditions (Greek, Jewish, Pauline, Dionysian, etc.)?

2. Consider something you recently experienced that was beautiful: how did that experience include Thomas Aquinas's three necessary features of beauty?

3. How does the intellectual component of beauty change the way you understand beauty and its power today?

4. How do the three approaches to beauty in this chapter relate to our late modern notions of faith?

5. How do the three approaches to beauty in this chapter relate to our late modern notions of reason?

6. How do the three approaches to beauty in this chapter provide substance for thinking about the relationship between faith and reason?

7. How does the idea that God is beauty itself transform the life of prayer? The life of study? The life of relationships of love?

6

THE THEOLOGY OF BEAUTY IN THE MODERN PERIOD

IF WHAT WE HAVE already examined constitutes the way beauty was conceived historically, then how is it that so much of how we understand beauty today differs from it? What happened between the Middle Ages and today that makes a theology of beauty seem strange to our aesthetic sensibilities? The short answer is that certain currents of thought arose that came to constitute a shift in the way that beauty was understood. In this chapter, we will examine some of the primary ingredients of that shift before turning our focus to the more relevant responses to this shift. More specifically, we will examine briefly the so-called modern turn to the subject and how, in the work of two primary modern philosophers Immanuel Kant and Alexander

Gottlieb Baumgarten, this had an effect upon conceptions of beauty. We will then examine the existential tradition's approach to beauty and the way that this tradition responds to this shift. In particular we will examine the work of two of the greatest existential thinkers, Søren Kierkegaard and Fyodor Dostoevsky. These developments in modern thought, we shall see, bear a continuity with much of the tradition we have examined already, while also introducing certain novelties.

THE MODERN TURN

Although there is never a single moment when one historical epoch transforms into another, scholars nevertheless attempt retrospectively to identify trends of thoughts or ideas in order to better organize and thus understand historical content. Historical events are used symbolically to express in a nutshell the way that these trends signal what is in reality a much slower and drawn out development. As we saw in chapter 4, many scholars mark the end of the ancient world with the moment that Justinian closed the Platonic Academy in 529, though other events are invoked by other scholars.

In a similar way, there are certain events that scholars point to in order to identify the transformation of the Middle Ages into what is now referred to as the Modern period, or Modernity. Some will invoke the movement known as the European Renaissance, others the period of exploration and colonialization, while others may be more specific and instead invoke, for example, the moment Martin Luther nailed his 95 theses to the door of the church at Wittenburg. What each event identifies, however, is the way in which the emergence of the Modern period is largely constituted by what is called the "turn to the self"—that is, the way in which Modernity saw a shift in collective interest and attention from the world inhabited by humanity to the human inhabitant herself. In this sense, the term "self" identifies an abstract first person perspective both collectively, in terms of society or culture, and individually. What this means is that whatever events may have contributed to it, the dawning of the Modern period was marked by human consciousness in process of becoming more aware of itself as a self—a human consciousness whose inward gaze becomes a lens through which to view the whole of reality.

Like all phenomena that constitute and inhabit human experience, beauty was both integral to and affected by the Modern turn to the self. Several scholars contributed to the place and role of beauty in this Modern turn, but none had more of an impact than Alexander Gottlieb Baumgarten (1714–62) and Immanuel Kant (1724–1804).

Known as the father of aesthetics, Baumgarten was the first to explore whether the human experience of the beautiful is governed by a mode of rational inquiry, or logic, all its own. In other words, he sought to understand how the human encounter with beauty might be rendered into something like a science unique in its own right and separate from other disciplines. The result of his search was the origination of the new "science" of aesthetics concerned with discerning what universal principles might constitute sensible knowledge. The goal of the science of aesthetics would be the perfection of the sensible cognition, that is to say, the perfection of that mode of knowledge associated with the senses. This perfection is what Baumgarten identified as the beautiful, which comes about largely as a result of aesthetic perception.[1] That is to say, the experience of beauty comes about through a series of sensible perceptions that, precisely in the act of being perceived, are held

1. Baumgarten, *Aesthetica*, Part I, §14–§20.

together in a kind of unity. Of course, there is much more to Baumgarten's achievements than space here allows us to discuss. What is important to note here, however, is the way in which after Baumgarten beauty becomes something primarily concerned with sense experience and subjective perception and is primarily transformed into "aesthetics."

One of the greats in the pantheon of Modern philosophers, Immanuel Kant followed a similar line of thought. Known for initiating what he himself called a "Copernican Revolution" of thought, Kant issued a paradigm shift in the Western intellectual tradition. Copernicus, as is well known, is credited with replacing a geo-centric model of the universe with a helio-centric model, prompting many of his posterity to describe it as a sort of revolution. Kant's use of this event to metaphorically describe his own thought had to do with the way that he replaces an "out there" approach to philosophical inquiry, in which philosophy begins with things in the world, with an "in here" approach that focuses instead on the conditions that allow thought to operate as it does. Within such conditions, beauty became reconfigured in significant ways.

Corresponding to Kant's paradigmatic shift in thought, beauty also shifted from being "out there" in things of the world to being "in here" within the subjective experience of the world. Yet it should be noted that, contrary to how he is often read by critics, he did not make beauty simply something subjective if by this one intends some kind of purely individualistic evaluation. Kantian subjectivity is not the naïve sense of detached individualism that subjectivity is often thought to be. Rather, it has to do with the common or shared sense of being subject to something transcendentally given, that is, something given from beyond the limits of human experience.

In his celebrated *Critique of Judgment*, the third critique within a trilogy that includes his *Critique of Pure Reason* and his *Critique of Practical Reason*, Kant provides an analysis of beauty from four interrelated "moments."[2] Each of these can be summed up by saying that, for Kant, beauty is that aspect of human experience in which something is enjoyed in such a way that the one enjoying it not only experiences the beautiful thing's "purposiveness" but also believes that this enjoyment of this beautiful thing is shared by all people despite not having a concept that verifies this. This may require some unpacking.

The second half of Kant's *Critique of Judgment* contains his critique of teleological judgment, that is, judgment about a thing's purpose, or end (*telos* in Greek). The thrust of his critique can be boiled down to establishing how human thought is incapable of finally determining a thing's purpose or end through our common modes of discursive, conceptual thought. No concept could contain the full sense of a given thing's end or purpose for which it was created. Nevertheless, when we experience a thing's beauty, Kant believed that we were experiencing its "purposiveness" even if we do not fully grasp its purpose.

When we like something, our liking carries no obligation for others to like that thing, which means that each human person is endowed with a personal sense of taste over which she holds almost complete dominion (we say "almost" because no human being's tastes are shaped outside of a socio-cultural influence). In contrast, so Kant believed, when we judge something beautiful our judgment carries at least an implied expectation that others must also judge the thing to be beautiful. In other words, a judgement of beauty bears an assumed universal validity, that is, valid for all people across time and space. However, any

2. See Immanuel Kant, *Critique of Judgment*, 43–95.

claim to universal validity can only be verified by means of a concept. In order for thoughts, ideas, and judgments to be seen as universally valid, they must be rendered communicable and intelligible to others. For something to be rendered communicable and intelligible, it must enter into what might be called "the shared economy of language" where concepts and categories enable thoughts, ideas, and judgments to pass from one mind to another. But beauty, so Kant believed, is unique in that it alone arrives by means of a judgment that bears universal validity without any concept. To put it bluntly, the beautiful, Kant maintained, is that which is liked by all people everywhere without a concept.

As can be seen, neither Kant nor Baumgarten can validly be accused of making beauty a purely subjective phenomenon. However, it is valid to recognize how their thoughts about beauty had the effect of making beauty much more dependent upon those subjective dimensions of human experience. With their emphasis on a certain kind of modern rationality, concepts, and categories, their thought occupies an esteemed place in the tradition of what is known as German idealism. Critics of this philosophical movement contend that its focus on the mind caused it to neglect important aspects of human experience and existence. Although its achievements were many, it also caused reactionary movements that were vital to the theological tradition of beauty. Perhaps no reaction was as vital and powerful as that which emerged out of the existential tradition.

THE EXISTENTIAL TRADITION

When one speaks of the existential tradition, one identifies something that is not easily reducible to a single definition or description. The term existentialism is often associated with a belief in meaninglessness, or lack of belief in God, or some other anxiety-based theme. Although it is true that many figures who could be classified as existential thinkers advanced ideas like these, it would be misleading to characterize the fundamental nature of existentialism in this way.

The best way to understand Existentialism is as a reaction to a particular impulse in philosophy that became widespread throughout much of the Modern period. Although diverse, this impulse was one that tended to prioritize those features of reality that were associated more with essences of things rather than things themselves. From its earliest origins, there has always been an important current of philosophical thought that sought the truth of things by focusing on what things all share in common. This shared common property is what a thing is, or what came to be called the thing's essence. Because essences are abstract, the forms of philosophy that focused on these tended also to be abstract and, for that reason, difficult, complicated, and to an extent unappealing to nonspecialists.

Existentialism in large measure arose as the reaction against those philosophical forms that, in the eyes of existentialists, were overly abstract and all too often had neglected those dimensions of human life that constitute the particularities of every day experience. Consequently, existential thought investigated experiences like boredom, anxiety, suffering, or loss, as well as moods, emotions, and various other phenomena that seem to be uniquely human.

Beauty was one such phenomenon that, in various forms, occupied a significant place among existential thought. Two existential thinkers in particular merit attention for the way in which beauty not only factored into their overall projects, but also for the unique way in which beauty was treated existentially. These figures—Søren Kierkegaard and Fyodor Dostoevsky—not only share an existentialist foundation to their thought, but for both beauty is given a central place therein. What one finds in their body of work is an approach to questions of existence that pushes the limits of thought beyond its abstract, discursive mode. It is, one might say, a kind of poetic thinking that not only explores the importance and nature of beauty in the world but that which itself flows out of the very intimacy of beauty and reason. This intimacy, as this book has argued, was at the heart of a theology of beauty.

SØREN KIERKEGAARD (1813–55)

If ever there was a thinker for whom the particular, concrete being served as the pinnacle of any philosophical or theological thought, it was the Danish thinker Søren Kierkegaard. One finds in the body of his work an account of beauty that bears explicit and implicit elements, both of which are unified in his central concern for the single, concrete individual. For Kierkegaard, beauty is realized in the experiences of desire, passion, imagination, even seduction, all of which open the individual to a dark other that must be confronted on the path toward a final threshold where the possibility of a leap of faith reveals itself.

Beauty is present throughout the entire journey toward the pinnacle of human destiny as religious faith in God. It is there in the earliest moments when the individual person awakens to the world through the colors, textures, sounds, etc., that constitute one's initial encounter with the world through sensuality. As this encounter awakens one to a conscious awareness of beauty, it also begins to provoke a reverence for that beauty manifest in an awareness that the world is good. In this awareness, an ethical response begins to emerge as the human person learns how to encounter and practice that good. Eventually, this aesthetic and ethical trajectory opens to the divine itself, where a religious response becomes urgent. However, this religious response is not one that can be mediated through any sort of universal, or commonly shared category (such as the kind provided through religions), even if the universal is involved. It must be something that the individual person confronts in his or her unique existence as an individual.

Even though it may not have been an explicitly conscious impulse in his thought, it is not difficult to detect in Kierkegaard's work a reawakening of St. Francis's desire to embrace the particularity of existence that enters the world in the Incarnation. Much like Francis, Kierkegaard sees in Christ the rupturing of all human attempts to transform existence into an abstract system of concepts and categories. As Terry Eagleton expresses it, for Kierkegaard "the crux of Christian faith, the Incarnation, is . . . the ruin of all reason."[3] The particular as particular can never be reduced to the commonality of universal concepts and categories, the instruments of human reason. Indeed, reason is ruined at the limits of the particular beyond which reason struggles more and more to filter particularity through its universal lens. Like Francis and others in the theological tradition of beauty, Kierkegaard sees the infinite value in the particularity of singular concrete existence, whose infinite value is revealed in the Incarnation when the Infinite itself enters into the finitude of particularity.

Christianity, which ought to be a continual cascade of effects flowing out of the Christ event, must resist every abstract reduction. Just as Christ stood silent before Pilate's question "what is truth?" (John 18:38) so too does Christianity fall silent when absorbed into the schemes of discursive intellectualism. Where Francis aspired to overcome

3. Eagleton, *Ideology of the Aesthetic*, 182.

certain modes of theological discourse that believed Christianity could thrive as an abstract system of thought as much as a concrete way of life, Kierkegaard understood his mission in a similar light.

A Christianity that has become removed from the concrete, so Kierkegaard maintained, becomes one more mode by which the universal unlawfully exercises its totality over the world. The universal, which most commonly takes the form of concepts and categories, may be necessary for thought to function. As primarily a construct of human thought, it carries the fragility of human limitations even if it is necessary for thought's operations. Nevertheless, it comes at a high cost: the flattening of the value of the particular individual into something that can only be seen for those aspects that are common to everyone and everything. The universal in this sense is a totalizing apparatus in that, by it, thought believes itself capable of grasping the whole. In reality, however, it is a whole that is constructed from only what is common leaving behind uniqueness and particularity. Christianity is nothing if not a revelation of the infinite value, and beauty, of the particular in Christ. "The object of faith," explains Kierkegaard, "is the actuality of the god in existence, that is, as a particular individual . . . as an individual human being."[4] Concepts, though helpful for understanding, do not in fact guarantee it, and nowhere is the truth of this more urgently revealed than in faith. "Even if someone were to transpose the whole content of faith into conceptual form," asserts Kierkegaard, "it does not follow that he has comprehended faith, comprehended how he entered into it or how it entered into him."[5]

It is all too common today to hear what might be called quantitative arguments against a personal God. Arguments

4. Kierkegaard, *Concluding Unscientific Postscript*, 326.

5. Kierkegaard, *Fear and Trembling*, Preface, 7.

such as these contend that, assuming there is a God, why would he care a whit about our puny, insignificant lives? If God is in fact the source and origin of all, why would a being of such immensity bother with beings like us who in comparison are as nothing. For Kierkegaard, ideas like these do not come from faith but rather derive from some other mode of universal thought that, for some strange reason, elevates the quantitative nature of the world to dictate who God can or cannot be. Instead, "faith is convinced that God is concerned about the smallest things."[6] Like beauty, love—especially the love that flows from God himself—not only does not need to obey quantitative measure, but defies it in every way. Faith for Kierkegaard is above all a manifestation of the beauty of particularity amidst a world that has become overconfident in the power of universals.

It would be shortsighted, however, to conclude that Kierkegaard rejected every form of universality. His was a way of thinking that dwelled, often uncomfortably, in between the particular and the universal. That he stressed the particular could be read as a strategy for remedying what he saw as a spectrum tilted too heavily toward the side of the universal, the side of essences. His account of beauty focused largely upon particularity but it did not neglect to include a place for the universal. One finds a correspondence between the two in his doctrine of repetition, which in many ways doubles as a doctrine of beauty.

The correspondence between beauty and repetition in Kierkegaard is explicitly stated: "Life is a repetition and . . . this is the beauty of life . . ."[7] He also calls repetition the "actuality and the earnestness of existence"[8] drawing together repetition, beauty, and being. Again, rather than remaining

6. Ibid., 34.

7. Kierkegaard, *Repetition Part I*, 132.

8. Ibid., 133.

abstract in his analysis, repetition and its beauty appears most concretely in the movement from the aesthetic to the ethical to the religious, a movement that is itself depicted in three symbolic figures.

Before looking to these three figures, however, it will be helpful to examine a bit more closely what Kierkegaard means by repetition and why it is the beauty of life. To begin, one need only pause a moment and ponder how much of one's day involves a repetition of the past. A person awakens, most likely engages in a morning routine, eats foods that are familiar, speaks words that have already been spoken, sees and hears many things that have already been seen and heard, etc. Yet somehow, amidst all this repetition, a newness continually breaks through allowing something that had not yet been experienced to arrive. Kierkegaard refers to this as the "dialectic of repetition": "for that which is repeated has been—otherwise it could not be repeated—but the very fact that it has been makes the repetition into something new."[9] Repetition, in other words, is both old and new, a comingling of the familiar and the unfamiliar. Somehow, it is this both/and, this comingling, that fills one's daily life with beauty.

Beauty's presence in this daily repetition takes many different forms, all of which begin with the aesthetic experience of sensual, immediate pleasure. This is where children, for example, first learn the good through comforting touches, savory foods, tranquil tones, etc. It is a form of beauty whose comforts can be difficult to move beyond in order to seek higher goods. The process of maturation requires ascending to higher forms of beauty and goodness, but often the pain of maturation can compel us to retreat into less noble forms of beauty and goodness; the repetition of familiar forms can be comforting. In such situations, the

9. Ibid., 149.

return of the familiar within repetition can elicit a pull so strong that it takes over a person's whole being in unhealthy ways. Nevertheless, repetition's beauty is such that there will always remain the possibility to glimpse the newness that calls within that repetition. It is this possibility that, for those mired in a state of unhealthy pleasure, carries them to the threshold where a leap becomes possible.

Kierkegaard uses three symbolic figures to illustrate this dynamic: the poet, the hedonist, and the seducer.[10] Each figure represents a particular encounter with the aesthetic mode of being, an encounter that pushes each to the threshold where a leap into the ethical and eventually religious modes of being, become more urgent and more feasible. In other words, for each figure, there is a strong desire to become religious though each of them go about it in the wrong way.

For the poet, the repetition of life begins as inspiration, as a beauty that beckons the poet into a poetic life. A great love fills the poetic heart as she ventures beyond the categorical where her imagination flies freely in the creation of her poetic world. She returns, however, to the real world to communicate in poetic form what she glimpsed in her imagination. Eventually, this causes a sense of melancholy to take hold as more and more, through the repetition, she realizes just how wide the gulf is between the imagined home of her longing and the actual world of her dwelling. Eventually, this melancholy itself becomes her

10. Each of these symbolic figures appears in varying texts. For the poet, see *The Point of View for My Work as an Author*, *Repetition*, and *Journals and Papers*; for the hedonist, see "The Immediate Erotic Stages of The Musical Erotic," in *Either/Or*; and for the seducer, see "The Diary of the Seducer," in *Either/Or*. For the taxonomy of these three figures in Kierkegaard's aesthetic cycle, I am indebted to Bruno Forte's short essay on Kierkegaard in *The Portal of Beauty: Toward a Theology of Aesthetics*, ch. 3.

home, her refuge even as it more and more loses any sense of real meaning. A kind of addiction to this melancholy is born in her because her very work as a poet flows from the ever-growing distance between that which she longs for but can never actually possess.

But repetition is the beauty of life, and no matter how deeply entrenched the poet may become in her melancholy, this beauty remains. At first this beauty was clear and fresh, the vision pursued by the poet. As the addiction to melancholy starts to take hold, however, this beauty withdraws, leaving its trace as an absence. The fiercer the addiction to this melancholy, the stronger becomes beauty's presence precisely in its absence! Repetition, then, pushes the poet to the brink where the desire for the beauty, lost as it is now in the melancholy but imposing itself in its absence, pushes the poet to the threshold where the leap of faith—that is, a leap into the beauty whose presence is conceived as an absence—becomes more and more urgent.

In a similar way, for the hedonist—represented by the figure Don Juan, a.k.a, Don Giovani—beauty is first glimpsed in a desire for pleasure and its eventual satisfaction. Through repetition, the hedonist comes to love the pleasure in itself rather than its satisfaction and ends up caught in a tragic cycle where she must move from pleasure to pleasure. It is a movement that becomes more and more dependent on the idea, or possibility, of pleasure rather than the actual pleasure itself. Eventually, the hedonist comes to find possibilities of pleasure more intense than their actuality, becoming enslaved by desire for desire's sake. The hedonist is then opened to the infinite restlessness of desire, spoken of so insightfully by Augustine when he wrote "Our hearts, Oh Lord, are restless until they rest in you," that nothing finite can satisfy.

Nevertheless, as with the poet, the beauty in desire's repetition remains as an absence. What first pleased the hedonist in the various experiences of pleasure was a beauty that now gradually withdraws as the hedonist becomes addicted to the desire itself. In its withdrawal, pleasure's beauty intensifies itself in its absence pushing the hedonist more and more into a state of anguish. At the point where the hedonist realizes the pleasures she seeks no longer satisfy the desire that has grown, the leap of faith becomes more and more urgent. It is a leap away from the endless pursuit of pleasure into the beauty that, although absent in the midst of the habits of hedonism, remains present as a glimmer of that which the pleasure once promised.

The third figure is the seducer, whose encounter with beauty begins in the self as that self is known in its relation to others. Like the hedonist, pleasure is involved insofar as the other becomes the source of the self's pleasure. But it is the beauty of oneself that the seducer sees reflected in the other. The seducer becomes addicted, as it were, to her own beauty insofar as that beauty appears within the pursuit of the person desired. Eventually, it is the pursuit itself, rather than the person pursued, that takes hold of the seducer who is now trapped in her own ego. Beauty remains necessary as the pull of the other, but it becomes distorted as that pull is relocated into the seducer's own ego.

As with the poet and the hedonist, the seducer's experience of beauty gradually becomes one of absence. The beauty that first appeared in the relation of love for another now withdraws as the seducer more and more falls in love with her own ego. All the while, beauty serves as the force of the seducer's desire, only the more that the seducer redirects this desire into herself, the more that beauty is experienced in its absence. As with the poet and the hedonist, the tension of the original desire for beauty now experienced as an absence brings the seducer to the threshold where a leap of faith is all that remains—a leap out of her own ego-centered life into a beauty that, though seemingly absent, remains as a call even in that absence.

What one finds with Kierkegaard's account of repetition in these three figures is a mode of beauty that is as much a both/and as repetition itself. Beauty is the original call, experienced as imagination, pleasure, and love. Yet in the every day experiences of melancholy, anguish, and loss that mark so much of human existence, this beauty withdraws itself to the degree that a person remains mired in the aesthetic mode of being. Only, much like Christ's sacrifice on the cross, by which he becomes absent so as to become present in a new way, it is a withdrawal by which beauty intensifies itself precisely by becoming more and more absent. It is as if through the forms that beauty takes in the imagination, pleasure, and oneself, one is elevated into the immense depth of beauty. Only in that depth her categories and concepts, malformed through the abuses of these forms as poet, hedonist, and seducer, can no longer mediate that beauty itself. She is left only with either the pain brought upon her by that abuse, or a leap beyond all categorical mediation into that depth of beauty where faith is the bond of love to God as Absolute.

The original experience of beauty dies in human sin yet remains ever present as a power to advance beyond the sin into a more ethical and eventually religious mode of being. It is a presence whose actualization requires the performance of repetition, a movement between old and new, familiar and unfamiliar. Beauty's power is manifest precisely in this repetition, which for Kierkegaard opens a person to the beauty that is there in faith.

FYODOR DOSTOEVSKY (1821—81)

Dostoevsky was not a philosopher or theologian in any conventional sense, a fact that serves to emphasize the root of his existentialism. Rather than composing works of systematic theology or philosophy Dostoevsky's existentialism is embedded within the Russian literary tradition. His was a narrative approach that believed the clearest way to express ideas and insights was within the lives of persons brought together onto a shared dramatic stage. The very power of his thinking, manifest with such passion within his pages, at the same time becomes challenging to pin down precisely because, as art, it invites continual interpretation, and for that same reason, contemplation. In his thinking expressed so eloquently in his many novels beauty penetrates through other various phenomena like truth, nothingness, suffering, and joy. Above all, beauty was made visible in the person of Jesus Christ.

Dostoevsky held a view of truth that was intimately bound up with beauty. So too was he keenly aware of the way truth in the Modern European paradigm had become distorted into what Rowan Williams describes as a "truth of defensible propositions, a truth demanding assent as if it were caused by facts."[11] This is not the kind of truth found in a life of faith because faith offers an entirely new way of seeing the world, a way that opens a person to the beauty at the depths of all creation. After having just been released from prison, where he had been incarcerated for alleged political subversion, Dostoevsky wrote a letter containing a personal statement of faith, in which he famously asserts, "if someone were to prove to me that Christ was outside the truth, and it was really the case that the truth lay outside Christ, then I should choose to stay with Christ rather than

11. Williams, *Dostoevsky*, 43.

the truth."[12] If Christ and truth are synonymous in some way, as Christians proclaim with John's Gospel (John 14:6), how can Dostoevsky's claim here be understood?

This is not so much a rejection of truth as it is a critique of what truth had become, indeed what truth of its nature always risks becoming. More than either the good or beauty, truth inhabits thought forms like concepts and categories wherein most human knowledge dwells. But precisely for this reason, it continually risks being reduced to finite constructs that can be more easily manipulated for human ends. "But man is so partial to systems and abstract conclusions," writes Dostoevsky, "that he is ready intentionally to distort the truth, to turn a blind eye and a deaf ear, only so as to justify his logic."[13] In choosing Christ over the truth, Dostoevsky exhibits a similarity with a Kierkegaardian account of faith that is willing to pass beyond, even die to, truth as analytic clarity of concepts and categories, a truth that has been reduced to a mere expression of human thought, and instead inhabit the truth of a God who dwells in life and death.

In contrast with a truth that is clear, definitive, and without mystery, beauty is ambivalent, murky, and ambiguous. It is, in a sense, freer to roam than either the good or the true. Goodness cannot dwell in evil any more than truth can dwell in error since each is the other's opposite. Yet beauty seems to obey no such law of opposites. Dmitri in Dostoevsky's magnificent *The Brothers Karamazov*—a character enslaved by his passions and self-indulgence—aptly explains:

> Beauty is a fearful and terrible thing! Fearful because it's undefinable, and it cannot be defined

12. See Jones, "Dostoevskii and Religion," 155–56.
13. Dostoevsky, *Notes from the Underground*, 23.

> because here God gave us only riddles. Here the
> shores converge, here all contradictions live to-
> gether . . . The terrible thing is that beauty is not
> only fearful but also mysterious. Here the devil
> is struggling with God, and the battlefield is the
> human heart.[14]

Beauty, as Dostoevsky conceives it within this complex character, does not abide a limit but shines its light as much in evil, disorder, indifference, dullness, and stupidity as in goodness, truth, order, attraction, and intelligence. Consequently, beauty can penetrate more deeply into the existence of what is real. In offering a fuller vision of something, beauty is a seeing of truth and a dwelling in the good. Beauty is the capacity to see beyond the appearance of things to their depth where they often hide themselves from a world suffering under the weight of sin.

Thus it is that beauty can be considered a crucified beauty for Dostoevsky. As that which carries within its very constitution all opposing forces, beauty imitates Christ upon the cross. As the God who suffers, Christ illuminates divine beauty in a world full of evil, suffering, and nothingness. It should come as no surprise that the life, and especially the death, of Christ become a focus for Dostoevsky. In Christ, God presents himself not in systematic, analytic form, but as a lived event, a character within the drama of human culture and society. As such, Christ is the divine response to the radical question of evil that confronts every human being: if we are created by a God of pure love, goodness, truth, and beauty how can we bear to live in a world that seems to be the very opposite, a world of sin, suffering, and evil? Christ therefore reveals a beauty that alone can bring the final triumph over evil and suffering.

14. Dostoevsky, *Brothers Karamazov*, Part I, Book III, chap. 3, 108.

If, in Dostoevsky's view, beauty provides the capacity to see to the depth of a given being, this is made possible to the fullest degree in and through Christ. Christ comes from the very depth to which all beauty points and from which all beings are born. In Christ, as Rowan Williams explains, "[w]hat is coming into focus gradually is the idea . . . that reconciliation with the unyielding and superficially meaningless processes which we confront becomes possible because of some event which reconfigures those processes as manifestations as gift or as beauty."[15] And this returns us to Dostoevsky's remark about the Christ who is outside the truth. Christ's beauty is a revelation of that which transcends the economy of mere cause and effect in the world. It is a beauty that, against all expectations breaks through the constructions of human thought to free persons from the strangle hold such constructions often impose.

Christ is for Dostoevsky the very presence of the divine love in a world that all too often senses its absence. Recall that Augustine saw love as the human experience of beauty, and beauty as the outward appearance of love. As God's love made visible Christ can be understood as the divine beauty expressing itself in a world of evil and suffering. This divine beauty is at the same time, then, a source of authentic meaning for concrete persons seeking more than the mundane matters that come to occupy human life. But it is a freedom not from these mundane matters but the freedom to see their beauty; that is, Christ's beauty is the power that frees human beings to see the divine beauty even in the seemingly mundane aspects of daily life. Again, Rowan Williams remarks on Dostoevsky's view of a love that frees us to see meaning:

15. Williams, *Dostoevsky*, 25.

> Meaning comes by the exercise of freedom—but
> not *any* sort of exercise of freedom. By taking the
> step of loving attention in the mundane require-
> ments of life together, something is *disclosed*.
> But that step is itself enabled by a prior disclo-
> sure, the presence of gratuity in and behind the
> phenomena of the world: of some unconditional
> love. The narrative of Christ sets that before us,
> and the concrete historical reality of Christ is
> what has communicated to human nature a new
> capacity for reflecting or echoing that love.[16]

Christ is the historical and therefore narrative evidence that
God dwells in the everyday, the mundane, and the simple.
He is the assurance that no life is without value no matter
how the world may come to measure what is or is not valuable precisely because his life illuminates the beauty in even
the most mundane. It is here that we can begin to see how,
as Dostoevsky famously wrote, beauty will save the world.

In his novel *The Idiot*, Dostoevsky attempted to present, in the character of Prince Myshkin, a perfectly beautiful
person and what most scholars believe to be a Christ-figure,
albeit a failed one. Myshkin is an orphaned young man,
exiled without a homeland and recovering from a severe
mental disorder. What one finds in this character, then, is
Dostoevsky's attempt to circumvent the difficulty of depict-
ing how beauty originates in persons bound by the time
and space of a fallen world.[17] In other words, Myshkin is
Dostoevsky's attempt to personify a beauty without beginning that gives itself without reserve to others, but more
importantly how such a beauty can only ever be an abstract
ideal in a fallen, sinful world.

16. Ibid., 44.
17. Ibid., 50.

Having just awoken from sleep during a dinner gathering, Ippolit, one of Myshkin's companions, announces, "'Is it true, prince, that you said once that "beauty" will save the world? Gentlemen!' he shouted loudly, addressing the whole company, 'the prince asserts that beauty will save the world! . . . What sort of beauty will save the world?'"[18] Many have taken this simple passage to mean that Dostoevsky believed beauty would in fact save the world. But to understand what this actually means requires understanding the context and characters whose dramatic narration gives the statement meaning.

As the character of Myshkin sought to capture, and as the theological tradition of beauty maintains, beauty is an excess, a surplus of formal, existential content that erupts into daily events to reveal something from a depth, something that seizes us, steals us away from ourselves, almost forcing us to look at ourselves in a new light. In entering into the fallen world of sin and suffering, this beauty, like Christ himself, risks being misunderstood and misused. The depth from which beauty comes and to which beauty points can be severed from the appearance it manifests. That is, seeing only the appearance, one can desire to seize and consume it rather than let oneself be seized and consumed by the fullness of beauty's excess and depth. Should that excess and depth continue to offer itself even amidst such seizure and consumption, as in the case of Christ himself, it ends up sacrificed upon the cross of human power.

So what could "beauty will save the world" mean? Dostoevsky offers no simple answer, but a few responses suggest themselves. First, a beauty that saves must be historical. Human beings are creatures who originate and form their identities within the flowing stream of time and the enduring stasis of shared space that appears as historical

18. Dostoevsky, *The Idiot*, 351.

narrative. Although beauty comes from a depth beyond all this, it is as nothing until it enters into this mysterious and often disconcerting flow of existence. Just as God could not be available to finite human knowing except through the distillation of time and space, so too is the beauty that redeems reliant upon, and at the mercy of, this same distillation.

Second, a beauty that saves must be linguistic, that is to say, must communicate itself from the depth where it dwells in fullness to the point of encounter with others. Although beauty is of its nature mysterious and, as Plato recognized, difficult, if it is to have saving power it cannot remain entirely shrouded in this mystery. While simultaneously preserving its mystery, it must speak itself in some way, even if such speaking is at the same time a revelation of a whole new way of speaking. In other words, it must enter into the economies of language constitutive of all otherness it touches.

Third, a beauty that saves is dramatic. It shines its glory in and with the vicissitudes of worldly drama rather than over and against it. Even if its shining at times hints at an order of tranquillity beyond the dramatic movements of a fallen world, it does so never at the expense of the world but instead reveals the value and meaning within the particular constituents of the world. It brings its order and harmony to the world, experienced at times as peace and at others as interruption, as much as it brings the world more completely into the order and harmony of its excess of being.

So, as with Kierkegaard, beauty for Dostoevsky is indeed a crucified beauty. Just as the world can only be redeemed by a God who enters into the furthest reaches of sin and suffering, so too does beauty bear this power within itself to appear in the furthest reaches of nothingness. Even when beauty's depth is sacrificed upon the cross of worldly power and personal desire, its capacity to resurrect itself in that power and desire is never extinguished. Beauty's call can never be silenced, but continues to reverberate even where ears have grown deaf.

DISCUSSION QUESTIONS

1. How are beauty and existentialism related?

2. Which traditions in the ancient and medieval period contribute most to the Kierkegaardian and Dosoevskian approaches to beauty and why?

3. How is the cross central to the approaches to beauty found in both Kierkegaard and Dostoevsky?

4. How might responses to the question "Is the cross of Christ beautiful?" differ when approached from our conventional late-modern notions of beauty, on the one hand, and when approached from the theology of beauty, on the other hand?

5. How does the theology of beauty provide resources for responding to the question, how will beauty save the world?

7

THE RETURN OF BEAUTY IN TWENTIETH-CENTURY THEOLOGY

As THIS BOOK HAS sought to illuminate, beauty has played an indelible and primary role throughout the Christian theological tradition. From its earliest origins well into the modern period, beauty has provided to human thought and practice a power that has not only opened human thought to the divine but sustained this relationship. Throughout our examination, we have seen beauty from a number of perspectives: as proportion, symmetry, harmony, fitting-ness, paraprosdokian, anagogical, analogical, parabolic, unity-in-plurality, simplicity, a gathering force, a plenitude of intelligibility, an emanational power, etc. Above all, beauty is the power that calls from beyond the limits of human thought, human perception, and human consciousness. In the modern period, as the last chapter briefly noted, there was a shift that led to the widespread notion that beauty is in reality something confined within the limits of human thought. Its status as a transcendent power that calls from beyond these limits was itself called into question. Much of our contemporary ideas and habits of mind concerning beauty are indebted to this Modern shift.

In this concluding chapter, we examine the return of beauty in twentieth-century theology with an eye toward understanding how such a return might carry with it significant content for a more flourishing community of thought and practice. There are many dimensions and a great deal of complexity involved in this return consisting as it does in the work of a number of figures. However, few figures are as significant to beauty's return in the twentieth century as the Swiss Jesuit Hans Urs von Balthasar. His work is as extensive and comprehensive as it is enriching and challenging. Although the primary currents of his thought flow out of the tradition of German idealism, his is at once an historical and metaphysical approach that embraces a multitude of figures and traditions. Von Balthasar will serve as the primary representative, then, for beauty's return in twentieth-century theology in the first part of this final chapter. His work is as formidable as it is comprehensive. In his immense corpus, one encounters a coalescence of so much in the Christian theological tradition (and beyond!) that it makes any attempt at summary not only difficult but risky. Nevertheless, in this chapter we will focus on some of the more primary themes in his theology of beauty selected not only for the broad significance they hold in his thought but also for the way they correspond to what we have already examined in the previous chapters.

HANS URS VON BALTHASAR (1905–88)

Upon their first encounter with von Balthasar's work, students are often surprised to learn that it is not considered strict, academic theology. One reason for this concerns the fact that his formal training was in the field of literature, though in a way that was steeped in the philosophical and theological traditions. Another reason is that he never held a university post, and so was not under any academic pressure with respect to publications. Nevertheless, his literary output remains one of the most prolific among scholars and academics today.

Educated in both the Benedictine and Jesuit traditions, he enrolled in the University of Zurich at the age of eighteen. At Zurich he studied primarily philosophy and German literature, which inspired him to eventually compose a doctoral thesis on German idealism. Around the same time, he entered the Society of Jesus, also known as the Jesuits, and pursued higher levels of philosophical studies. During this time, he came into contact with Erich Przywara (pronounced ER-ik SHVA-ra), who introduced him to the *analogia entis*, the "analogy of being." This would prove to be a foundational principle for all of von Balthasar's efforts, a principle that is as complex as it is controversial. We will examine this more closely a bit further along.

While a student, he struck up friendships with many others who would become influential scholars in their own right, including Jean Daniélou and Henri de Lubac. Both figures (and others) contributed to von Balthasar's love for the Fathers of the Christian tradition, eventually inspiring him to compose works on Maximus the Confessor and Gregory of Nyssa. Von Balthasar also had a deeply personal and scholarly relationship with the foremost Protestant theologian of the twentieth century, Karl Barth. Barth's work in many ways centralized for von Balthasar the role of beauty and attraction in the life of faith and its theological expression. But apart from these scholars, the single most important influence on von Balthasar was the medical doctor and mystic Adrienne von Speyr. Her visions became for von Balthasar a source of inspiration and evidence for the theological positions he would eventually come to espouse.

The return of beauty as a theological theme could be said to really take off with the publication of von Balthasar's seven-volume *Herrlichkeit*, translated as *The Glory of the Lord*. This is the first part of a massive three-part trilogy consisting also of the *Theo-Drama* and the *Theo-Logic*, treating most fundamentally the good and the true respectively. Even though the divisions within this trilogy might appear to suggest that beauty occupied only one of the three parts, in reality beauty penetrates all three parts in various ways. This is because for von Balthasar, beauty is the beginning, the first word that alone can ensure that attraction and mutual indwelling of the good and the true. Von Balthasar explains this relationship as well as the importance that beauty has within the world's self-understanding:

> Beauty is the word that shall be our first. Beauty is the last thing which the thinking intellect dares to approach, since only it dances as an uncontained splendour around the double constellation of the true and the good and their inseparable relation to one another. Beauty is the disinterested one, without which the ancient world refused to understand itself, a world which both imperceptibly and yet unmistakably has bid farewell to our new world, a world of interest, leaving it to its own avarice and sadness.[1]

1. Balthasar, *Glory of the Lord*, 1:19.

At the heart of von Balthasar's project is the idea that beauty is present everywhere and at all times throughout reality. This "transcendental" status of beauty alone enables the relation between the good and the true to sustain itself. Not only, then, is beauty one of existence's transcendental properties, it is the primary mode through which existence makes itself known and knowable.

The remainder of von Balthasar's project is in large part dedicated to unpacking the various layers and implications of what all this means. As can be expected, this unpacking results in a number of themes and ideas that become central to his project. Examining the most significant of these will help us begin to see the contours of beauty's resurrection in twentieth-century theological thought.

BEAUTY AS FORM

Sight is a power given to almost all sentient creatures. There is a freedom that comes with the capacity to perceive objects in time and space, and creatures that are gifted with sight are better able to negotiate with their surroundings than creatures that are not. But it is evident that the capacity to see differs even among creatures who possess it as a power. A creature like a bird, for instance, has the capacity to see with a wider perspective than human beings and birds of prey have a capacity to see that is eight times more powerful than human sight.

For the human being the act of seeing is much more than a physical sense. Rather, seeing begins in the physical sense of sight, but what is seen enters into, or is taken in by, a process that opens both the seer and the seen to a depth that otherwise remains hidden from view. A being's depth, which is not obvious in its outward appearance, is what von Balthasar called a thing's form, and it is the primary instance of beauty.

Von Balthasar followed the classical and medieval notion that God is in Himself an excess of form, a plenitude of intelligible content that as a plenitude is too much to fit into human categories and concepts. As the excess of all formal content, God gives himself to be known in the form of all beings that constitute the created order. God's form, which is God's beauty, can never finally be reduced to human concepts and categories even if it gives itself in bite size pieces, so to speak, to human cognition. Thus, every being that exists shares in the divine form but in its own unique, singular way; that is to say, to be a creature means to have form and therefore to be beautiful.

Form, therefore, is itself an appearance of Being's depth, the plenitude of the origin out of which all that exists comes forth. In coming forth, the depth of being is contracted into the form of this or that particular being, and each particular being is a unique, unrepeatable moment through which the plenitude of being shines itself. Seeing this depth is no simple task but requires developing one's capacity to "see the form"—one of Balthasar's most significant principles—of things beyond their mere appearance. Indeed, von Balthasar's theological project involves discovering the ways in which theology can serve to teach people how to see the form of a being, and in seeing the form, see the divine presence therein.

However, such seeing is not solely the task of the one who sees. As the divine beauty giving itself in a finite way, the form bears in itself a power to see. "The essence of form," explains Louis Dupré remarking on Balthasar's theory of form, "lies not in its being a potential object of sense perception, but rather in its intrinsic power *to express*—whatever mode of appearance that expression may take."[2] The expression of form requires a corresponding material principle. Getting beyond the dualism that a form/matter couplet can often provoke, however, Balthasar contends that a thing's form is precisely its capacity to express itself as "this being." A being's appearance in the material world derives from its formal power to express itself as a phenomenon in the world. "This phenomenal form of the entity," writes von Balthasar, "is the way it expresses itself; it is a kind of voiceless, yet not inarticulate speech."[3] Although always distinct, a being's form and matter are never separable: its matter appears as it does by virtue of its form's power to express it as such. What one perceives as beautiful in any being is the form as expressive power.

If beauty is the formal depth of being that presents itself in various beings, and if it is a being's form that is perceived, then beauty bears in itself a revelatory capacity. That is to say, beauty communicates truth with a greater capacity to engage the whole person than mere data or information can. As von Balthasar puts it, "[beauty] brings with it a self-evidence that enlightens without mediation."[4] In other words, beauty touches the intellect in an immediate way that does not require a concept or category but that, even without these cognitive apparatuses, remains intelligible to the various modes of human cognition. It is an intelligibility, however, more akin to intuition than to discursive thought, at least in its initial perceptibility.

BEAUTY AS EXPRESSIVITY

And so the beauty of any and every given being is its form, which rather than identifying some "thing" within the being

2. Dupré, *Religious Mystery and Rational Reflection*, 70.

3. Balthasar, *Epipologue*, 59.

4. Balthasar, *Glory of the Lord*, 1:37.

identifies its capacity to express. There is, then, an intimate association in von Balthasar's thought between beauty and expressivity, which means that examining its various dimensions has the added benefit of providing clearer vision of how he configures beauty. Expressivity, however, identifies the power that manifests itself in expression, which is the way in which expressivity enters the world of concrete activity. Thus, the examination of expressivity is best pursued by examining concrete expression.

First, expression is an act that always presupposes some other for whom the expression is intended. This is not to say that expression is not also an act undertaken for the one expressing. Rather, it is to emphasize that even the "for oneself" of all expressive acts requires the counterpart of the "for some other" if the act is to have any effect or reality. Human beings are creatures that share a common nature, and in Balthasar's view this means that one's identity as a self can only ever emerge into greater fullness as it finds itself in others. Expression is always mutually inclusive as it can only ever take place within the movement between a self and an other. Real beings find completion in one another, explains von Balthasar, precisely because the greater degree of completion that all expression intends arrives only in its appearance *for* some other.

Second, expression is not only an act through which a given being comes into appearance, but it is an act through which a given being aspires to reveal, albeit in small doses over the span of a lifetime, its own plenitude of intelligible content, or "subsistence." Recall that for Dionysius and the scholastic thinkers he influenced, God as beauty identified both God's appearance in and as the world but also God's hiddenness that remains forever veiled. To put it another way, every revelation of appearance is also simultaneously a revelation of an excess that hides itself behind the appearance. For von Balthasar, this is as true for creatures as for God. "Because someone who expresses himself is always something more than his expression," he explains, "he remains veiled to me in his subsistence even as he is a person truly expressing and unveiling himself."[5] The reason for this concerns the nature of communication: as a qualitative rather than quantitative exchange, communication requires not only something given, but also that the giver preserve herself as giver. The word "preserve" here does not mean withholding oneself, but rather the very possibility of the act of self-giving—one can only give insofar as one's integrity as a giver remains intact or preserved. Since all expression concerns preservation in this sense, all expression is an appearance of a being's excess of substance, which, as an excess, is the being's very rootedness in its divine origin, its "innerness" as von Balthasar calls it.

Third, beauty as expressivity points to a being's "innerness." Caution should be taken here: beauty as inner expressivity does not mean that a being first becomes consciously aware of herself and, in this awareness, becomes able to communicate, or express, this innerness to some other. Rather innerness identifies the capacity to impart oneself to another, which, as von Balthasar explains, implies a mysterious "partition" "in" another. That is to say, a being's beauty as an expression of innerness is a giving of oneself over to another with the consequence that the one expressing makes itself—that is its innerness, its subsistence, its spiritual depth—real in the world. In von Balthasar's own words, a being "proceeds out of itself by virtue of a dynamic given to it in order to real-ize itself (its innerness) in the very act of expressing."[6] Expressivity is as much a giving

---

5. Balthasar, *Epilogue*, 52.
6. Ibid., 51.

over to another as it is a making real, or "real-izing" of one-self in the world.

Finally, beauty as expressivity concerns the crucial theme of recognition. As can be discerned already in the preceding, expressivity is both a giving over to another and a receiving of oneself in the very process. Expression, therefore, is not only an act whereby one gives oneself to another but also the act of receiving another's self-expression. Receiving another's expressive content does not mean taking hold of it. Instead, it means being-taken-hold-of by that appearance as I bring it into my innerness. The capacity to "take in" the appearance of the other requires that I gather up the variety, diversity, or plurality of the other's being as it is expressed to me. It is a diversity, variety, or plurality of shapes, colors, textures, ideas, thoughts, motions, sounds, etc. My ability to perceive all these as a unity—what von Balthasar calls "apperception"—rather than merely seeing each aspect in singular isolation, derives from the unity that constitutes the power of apperception, that is to say, the unity out of which my apperception flows.

When I apperceive another's expression I am caught up in beauty and become a recipient of the beautiful. This is important to underscore since it means that my apperception is not a willed synthesis of the variety of impressions. Instead, in receiving the beautiful I grasp the fullness of a thing as it appears from out of its depth. Beauty provides the power, then, to unify the otherwise multiform elements involved in the expression itself. From this it follows that this other "is a reality I am thus able to recognize on the basis of my own reality."[7] Von Balthasar referred to this power as a being's *Gestalt*. As he himself explains it, *Gestalt* "is the unity encountering the perceiver that is also simultaneously manifest in the experience of self . . . so that the object

7. Ibid., 52.

encountered and the 'I'—in spite of the variety of our ever-unique essences—truly communicate in the all-one depth of reality."[8] *Gestalt* identifies the way in which beauty comes near to a being to give a real encounter with the depth of being as this depth gives itself by means of particular beings. It is, one might say, the very form of expressivity as it is encountered in the expressions of beings.

One's capacity to recognize other expressions and self-expressions in the world is in large measure dependent upon one's own mode of expression. And since expression is most fundamentally a giving of oneself over to another, it follows that one's capacity to recognise the world and all that is in it is directly bound up with the degree to which that one gives of herself in expression. One receives what the world offers in direct proportion with the way in which one gives oneself to the world.

In this sense, one finds in von Balthasar's notion of expression a coalescence of many of the classical features of beauty. Expression is a light in which a being comes to appearance and therefore comes to greater completion in its being. By virtue of its appearing, a being's expression is a communication of its beauty both for itself and for another. The community of beauty, of beautiful beings, can then be understood in the sense of a Dionysian hierarchy: as a community of expressivity that is involved in both self-expression and—in proportion to the degree of that self-expression—recognition of and participation in others' expressions. Since expressivity is a "pouring out," so to speak, of "innerness" it gestures toward beauty as a plenitude of intelligible content, which content constitutes the very substance of a given being. Again, in ways reminiscent of Dionysius and the scholastic thinkers, a being's substance, although never relinquishing its status as belonging

8. Ibid., 63.

to this unique being, is only completed or perfected as it is given to others. At this point, we are confronted by another of von Balthasar's significant themes: beauty as analogy.

BEAUTY AS ANALOGY

There is probably no principle that better captures the intimacy between reason and beauty than that of analogy. Upon hearing the word "analogy" most people today conceive of some poetic or literary device that compares one thing to another, or attempts to make some notion more intelligible by locating it within the relationship of two other notions/terms/ideas. When used philosophically or theologically, however, analogy is not only more complicated but its application is much more extensive.

To put it concisely, analogy is a principle that identifies the mutual interpenetration or harmonious togetherness of unity and diversity, of identity and difference. The historical roots of this principle could be traced back to the earliest versions of the call examined in chapter 1: a call issues from a source other to the hearer, yet, as a call that is heard, the call unites caller and hearer together without blurring their distinctions. One might trace this principle to the origins of the trinitarian nature of God in the Christian tradition. The revelation that God is a trinity—three divine persons manifesting one divine nature—could only have been received upon a foundation that did not oppose the one to the many, unity to diversity, or identity to difference but instead understood them as existing one for the other. In other words, the trinitarian nature of God as three persons sharing one divine nature does not posit a fourth thing—the divine nature—behind the three persons but rather identifies that the divine nature *is* the three persons in perfect communion.

Wherever one wants to locate the origins of the principle of the analogy, however, one of its first formal authoritative expressions occurs at the Fourth Lateran Council in 1215. In the second Constitution, which addressed the errors of Joachim of Fiore on the trinitarian nature of God, the Council rendered the following statement: "For between creator and creature there can be noted no similarity so great that a greater dissimilarity cannot be seen between them."[9] If God is in fact the creator of the natural world and all that is in it, then it follows that every entity bears the stamp of the divine being. Creatures, then, in coming from the creator bear a similarity to their creator making them communications of God discernible to human reason. However, as this Lateran principle asserts, whenever similarities are recognized they not only convey something held in common, but more importantly they also reveal the contrast of dissimilarity. When discerning attributes of God from creatures one must always bear in mind that, as Augustine famously asserted, if you can think it, it is not God. From this it follows that the whole of existence is an interweaving of unity and diversity, identity and difference, similarity and dissimilarity.

Although present in Aquinas's metaphysical theology, von Balthasar draws his own account of the analogy of being from his teacher Erich Pryzwara. Pryzwara first introduces the foundation of his configuration of the analogy of being, what he refers to in his work as the *analogia entis,* with deference to the Augustinian declaration of the "God in us, God beyond us." This declaration identified Pryzwara's fundamental intention to think the "ultimate" relation between God and creatures. The God "in us" identified

9. The full textual content from this council can be found online at http://www.papalencyclicals.net/Councils/ecum12–2.htm#Confess ion of Faith.

the omnipresent, omniscient, and omnipotent God who comes near in person and who works and guides all things. The God "beyond us" identifies the absolute difference and separation of God's plenitude of substance that remains forever beyond all of creation. Hence, the *analogia entis* was a way of thinking and speaking what, for Pryzwara and von Balthasar, signified the most fundamental event of all existence: that the shared unity of being common to all creatures at once also bears in itself the radical diversity of differences among beings.

It might help to further illuminate the nature of the *analogia entis* by examining one of the most famous (or infamous, perhaps) misreadings of it in twentieth-century theology. The foremost Protestant theologian of this time was, as noted above, Karl Barth, with whom von Balthasar developed a close, personal relationship. It was a friendship based not only on common interests but also on disagreements and divergences. The most famous of these arose when Barth, commenting on the *analogia entis*, called it the "invention of the anti-Christ" and the "only good reason for not becoming a Catholic." As Barth understood it, the *analogia entis* identified a perverse sort of natural theology that allowed creatures to relate—albeit analogically—to God by means of a broader, shared category of being common to both God and creatures. Within this sort of understanding, Barth's rejection of the *analogia entis* is not only valid but necessary: for if it is believed that there is a broader category of being common to both God and creatures, then God is reduced to one instance of being— albeit supernatural being, but being nonetheless—which is the same being shared by creatures. Even though creatures experience being in a natural way and God experiences it in a supernatural way, "natural" and "supernatural" in this reading become merely two species of a higher common genus, the common sharing of which allows a crossing over from one to the other, so to speak, without problem.

Obviously such a conclusion is theologically troubling for a number of reasons: God is no longer "that than which nothing greater can be thought," as St. Anselm of Canterbury had put it in the eleventh century, but instead becomes one more instance of a now higher and more powerful being that contains both God and creatures. Consequently, both God and creatures can be thought by means of an inquiry into being; because being is shared in common between God and creatures, creatures can get ahold of and possess God conceptually and categorically. God's transcendence is no longer an absolute transcendence but rather a transcendence that is reducible to being. That is, inquiry into being is now thought to provide authentication of God's existence or lack thereof. God is somehow thought to live and move and have his being within a sphere whose rules and laws are also common to both God and creatures. When being is a higher and common category shared by God and creatures, the kind of atheism that erupts in the late modern period is hardly surprising.

Von Balthasar was tireless in his efforts to convince Barth that he had misunderstood the nature and intention of the *analogia entis*. In fact, it is the *analogia entis* that prevents the theological conclusions noted above from ever becoming possible. The conclusion that Barth had drawn about the *analogia entis* actually identifies what in the philosophical tradition is referred to as a "univocal" understanding of being: being is the "one voice" (univocal), or single voicing of being, that contains creatures and God. The scholastics of the Middle Ages, for the most part, had rejected such a univocal predication of being as theologically unsound, much for the same reasons noted in the above problems to which it gives rise.

In rejecting a univocal configuration of being, another option reveals itself, and it is one that critics of Barth often attribute to him in some form. Rather than sharing being in common, perhaps God and creatures are so divided such that there is nothing whatsoever in common. This conclusion, referred to as an "equivocal" understanding of being, absolutizes the difference between God and creatures to the point of denying any and every possibly mode of unity. In an effort to safeguard the divine transcendence, God is pushed so far away from creation that creation of itself has no recourse for knowing God. God can only speak himself to a creation whose capacity to hear God's speaking is also entirely dependent upon that very speaking.

Just as they rejected the univocal understanding of being, most of the scholastic thinkers of the Middle Ages rejected this alternative. Rather than reducing God to another being among beings, the equivocal option rendered a God who is aloof, disconnected, and completely out of reach. Under such conditions, what purpose could there be in worship, prayer, or liturgy? What remains to provide human thought with any measure for true and false conclusions about God? When nothing is thought to be in common between God and creatures, then knowledge of God seems impossible.

In between these two ways of understanding the relationship between creatures and God, *analogia* affirms at one and the same time *both* the unity between God and creatures necessary for knowledge and love of God *and* the difference between God and creatures necessary for God to be God and creatures to be creatures—a difference that is equally necessary for knowledge and love of God. Even more, as it is found in the work of Pryzwara and von Balthasar after him, *analogia* affirms a direct proportion between the unity and difference such that any unity is always accompanied by a far greater difference (as proclaimed by the Fourth Lateran Council). As a principle, the *analogia entis* requires one to think at the very same time both unity and diversity, identity and difference. As von Balthasar conceives it, the difference/diversity of being is itself revealed in and through the unity/identity of being, and the unity/ identity of being comes more and more into appearance in the encounter with being's differences/diversities. Indeed, without both one inevitably falls into either univocal or equivocal configurations, both of which render unhappy conclusions.

It would not be overstating the matter to suggest that for von Balthasar, the beauty of being is most intensely concentrated and most visibly illuminated when viewed through the lens of the *analogia entis*. For this reason it is perhaps most appropriate to speak of it in the language of the *event* of being's analogy. It is an event because, in every particular being's act of existing, unity comes together with diversity, identity with difference, and in this coming together the beauty of being announces itself. Being is not some "thing" that becomes discernable and comprehensible through correct categories and concepts. Rather, it is a happening where unity gives itself in diversity and difference, and where diversity and difference approach an always-arriving unity.

It might be worthwhile to pause for a moment here and ask how it is that von Balthasar comes to the conclusion he does about the *analogia entis*; that is, what is it that legitimizes this principle and its universal applicability? Is this a principle that comes from the history and development of human thought itself, that is to say from the tradition of philosophical inquiry? Or is this something that derives from the deposit of faith as revealed by God? As might be expected, the answer is more both/and than it is either/or.

In one sense, the *analogia entis* is a principle that, from the earliest period of philosophical inquiry up to its explicit expression within scholastic thought, had always been gestating in the womb of the Western intellectual tradition. Initiating one of the most well-known and well-rehearsed conflicts in philosophical thought, the pre-Socratic philosophers had debated whether being as such is a static permanence or whether it was eternal flux and change. Parmenides of Elea (c. 550 BCE), espousing a position of absolute identity, held that being is permanence, a static presence whose changes and transformations are merely illusions. In contrast, Heraclitus of Ephesus (c. 535–475 BCE), advancing a position of absolute difference, argued that it was in fact the static permanence of being that was illusory. Rather, being is nothing other than flux, change, and alteration, for as he famously declared "no one steps into the same river twice." It could be said that these two positions, held together, set the parameters wherein the principle of being as an analogy could reveal itself.

Plato was one of the first to propose a solution to this apparent conflict with his doctrines of the ideal forms and participation. Following Heraclitus, Plato maintained that the world of change and difference is indeed real, that things do not merely appear to change but in fact do change. However, following Parmenides he also affirmed that the world of change is but a shadow that points beyond itself to the realm of real being where ideal forms exist in an unchanging and eternal way. Bringing these two dimensions together, Plato maintained that all finite beings we experience in the world, then, participate in their ideal forms, which exist somehow independently of their finite forms. To put it another way, finite things are images of their more real archetypes, which exist in the truest sense of the term.

Aristotle conceived of analogy as both a mode of speech and a fundamental feature of being even though he does not explicitly use the word "analogy" when discussing being. What he does say is that "being can be said in many ways" and he uses the example of health to establish his point. There are many ways in which a given thing can be "healthy": medicine is called "healthy" because it is the cause of health; urine is called "healthy" because it is a symptom of health; and a person is "healthy" as the primary instance of health that can measure all other instances. His point is that all such uses are valid because "healthy" is said in many ways. Like "healthy," "being" is also said in many ways. This principle further entails that these many ways of "being" are not held by some more primordial principle of uniformity since, if there was such a principle, it too would have to "be" and would consequently be another way in which being is "said." Rather, being is certainly a unity in itself, but a unity whose unifying force emerges with difference and diversity. With this principle it becomes possible to see how there was an analogy with respect to being in Aristotle's thought.

In this way, Greek thought became a foundation for later elaborations of analogy. It enters into the Christian theological tradition in a number of different ways, both implicitly and explicitly. It is possible to think of it as a natural counterpart to the doctrine that, as Trinity, God is a unity in plurality, an identity in difference. It is this correspondence that enables von Balthasar to identify Jesus Christ, in whom the perfect union of God and the world becomes visible and concrete, as the personal manifestation of the *analogia entis*.

CHRIST: THE BEAUTY OF THE *ANALOGIA ENTIS* MADE PERSONAL

The theology of beauty has always been bound up with the trinitarian person of the Son and his Incarnation in the human nature of Jesus of Nazareth. As we saw in the work of Thomas Aquinas, beauty is most closely associated with the Son who is the express image of the Father. The existential tradition also emphasized the role of the crucified Christ in approaching the beauty of God. Von Balthasar's own approach to theological aesthetics can be read as a culmination of all associations between beauty and the Son. His primary configuration of this association happens according to the *analogia entis*: Christ the Son who becomes human in Jesus personifies the *analogia entis*; that is to say, in the person of Jesus Christ the beauty communicated in the *analogia entis* is made human.

As we have seen, from its origins the theology of beauty has maintained that God is beauty itself. As the plenitude of all that is, was, and will be, God is the one in whom everything is expressed. Expression, in von Balthasar's theological aesthetics, involves a giving of oneself over in expressibility, a self-surrender that reveals the depth behind appearance. It is within this context where von Balthasar locates the person of the Son: "In God himself the total epiphany, self-surrender, and self-expression of God the Father *is* the Son, identical with him as God."[10] In other words, the Son has his identity in and as the expressibility of the Father, which is to say that in Jesus the Son "is the adequate sign, surrender, and expression of God within finite being."[11] In the person of the Son, who John's Gospel proclaims is "the truth" itself, all that is true in the world "is held together"

10. Balthasar, *Epilogue*, 90.
11. Ibid., 89.

(Col 1:17). As von Balthasar explains, however, this is only possible if the very being of the Son in his assumption of a human nature in Jesus is the *analogia entis* itself.

The point at stake here concerns how human thought and practice might be capable of holding together the two fundamental features of a theology of beauty. On the one hand, the claim that in the beautiful things of the world, and especially in its most comprehensive reality of all that human beings know, namely being itself, God communicates his very own divine being. On the other hand, that at the same time God reveals his divine beauty in the beautiful things of the world, God stands above and beyond all worldly being in his divine beauty, wherein resides his absolute freedom. It is solely by virtue of this divine freedom that God can also make use of being itself to reveal his "inconceivably free turning to us" on his own terms. In the Son's assumption of a human nature, God reveals this "turning to us" in a way that not only reveals the limits of how human thought might attempt to approach it, but also that God's freedom residing beyond the limits of human thought may also be communicated in being itself.

To say that the Son in Jesus is the *analogia entis* is to say that he embodies in his person both the identity and difference in God the Father. Insofar as the Son is God himself, Jesus as the Incarnation of the Son reveals his identity with God. But insofar as the Son is eternally begotten and so distinct from the Father, Jesus reveals divine difference itself; that is to say, Jesus reveals difference as a divine attribute. As von Balthasar puts it, Jesus reveals the "transcendence over what we think of as identical,"[12] and consequently he reveals the nature of transcendence as such. It is by virtue of the revelation in Jesus Christ that the transcendentals themselves—the good, the true, and

12. Ibid., 92.

the beautiful—can be identified with God's divine being. In the same way that the divine essence is not some fourth thing communicated in the three persons of the Trinity, so neither are the transcendentals merely the manifestation of a fourth divine life. Rather, the three persons of the Trinity quite simply are the divine eternal life in procession. In the same way, the transcendentals, all identical with each other, are also identical with the manifestation of the inner divine life as procession. To use a crude analogy, it is similar to the various states in which two atoms of hydrogen and one atom of oxygen can appear. Ice, steam, and water do not reveal some fourth thing called "H_2O" behind each form. Rather, each form is a manifestation of H_2O; they are all identical with the compound itself.

As the *analogia entis* manifest in the form of a person, Jesus embodies all the principles of a theology of beauty. Much of this point was explained in chapter 2. Jesus calls people to himself, and so embodies the divine *kalon* that was examined in chapter 1. It is a call that is a manifestation of symmetry, harmony, and proportion insofar as the call issues from the particularity of Jesus as a person in time and space and echoes to other persons in their particular occupations of time and space. In other words, the Incarnation is not God's attempt to become some universally rational category to be mapped onto the lives of those to whom he calls. Rather, the divine beauty—as a plenitude of intelligibility—enters the particular, concrete momentum that defines human life. By virtue of its plenitudinous excess, divine beauty is able to fit with every particularity without ever flattening itself into a universal.

It is a call that is also a unity-in-plurality in that even though it calls each person in his or her particularity, it is a call that constitutes an ever-increasing body of believers. The twentieth-century French Jesuit, and friend of von Balthasar, Henri de Lubac aptly captures this unity-in-plurality when he asserts that "Christ loves us individually but not separately,"[13] which means insofar as Christ's love is the very power of salvation, we can validly repurpose this statement to read: "Christ saves us individually but not separately." Christ is the very form of salvation, which is a form that is one and many, individual and plural. It consists of its own singular identity that is constituted in the difference of otherness.

Emphasizing the Augustinian dimension of beauty, von Balthasar also reads the Son's incarnation in Jesus as the existence in, by, and through which the triune love of God is made real in the world. Recall that Augustine had maintained that beauty is love made visible, while love is the inner, spiritual experience of beauty. The Son's assumption of a human nature in the person of Jesus is the most visible form that love can take. Moreover, it is a love that reaches its culmination when it "has allowed every form of sinful non-love to vent itself on him. By taking on everything that rebels against God, he buries it in death and the grave."[14] By virtue of this power that resides in him as the most intense appearance of love, he is also able to unify in himself the various forms of love that appear to us as contrary even to the point of opposition. All contradictions and oppositions are already transcended and reconciled in his form because it is a form whose very substance is the plenitude of all formal content.

As this final chapter has sought to demonstrate, it is possible to speak of a return of beauty in twentieth-century theological discourse thanks in large part to the work of Hans Urs von Balthasar. Even though he was not alone in his efforts, the immense body of literature that he produced not only makes him the most important representative of

13. Lubac, *Splendor of the Church*, 45.

14. Balthasar, *Epilogue*, 94.

the general twentieth-century return of beauty in theological thought, but it establishes him as one of the foremost, if not the foremost, leader of this return. Given the immensity of his literary output it is difficult to single out any one dimension of his theology of beauty as being the most important. Therefore we have examined a varied array of dimensions, each of which constitute the fundamental force of his theology of beauty, or theological aesthetics.

DISCUSSION QUESTIONS

1. In what ways can von Balthasar's theology of beauty provide resources for the various theological problems (the existence of God, the relation between church and state, the complexity of religious belief, speaking about God, etc.) confronting our late-modern world?

2. How does von Balthasar's notion of form compare with Albert's notion of form?

3. In what ways does von Balthasar's notion of "expressivity" identify with and differ from how we today think of art as expressive?

4. How can the *analogia entis* help us discern between various images/models of God today?

5. Defend the thesis, "according to the Christian tradition, a theology of beauty is inseparable from the *analogia entis*."

6. What is the relationship between von Balthasar's approach to beauty and the other primary traditions that we've looked at in this book?

7. What are some significant difference and similarities between von Balthasar's theology of beauty and your own approach to beauty?

BIBLIOGRAPHY

Albert the Great. *Summa De Bono*. In *Albert the Great, Opera Omnia*, tom. 28, edited by H. Kühle, C. Feckes, B. Geyer, and W. Kübel. Monasterii Westfalorum: Aschendorff, 1951.

Aquinas, Thomas. *Commentary on the Divine Names of Dionysius the Areopagtie*. Edited by C. Pera. Turin-Rome: Marietti, 1950. No English translation as of November, 2015.

———. *Summa Theologica*. Translated by the Fathers of the English Dominican Province. Einsiedeln: Benziger Brothers, 1947.

Aristotle. *Metaphysics*. Edited by W. D. Ross. Oxford: Clarendon, 1924.

———. *Nichomachean Ethics*. Translated by H. Rackham. Volume 19 of *Aristotle in 23 Volumes*. Cambridge: Harvard University Press, 1934.

———. *On the Heavens*. Translated by W. K. C. Guthrie. London: W. Heinemann, 1945.

———. *Poetics*. Edited by R. Kassel. Oxford: Clarendon, 1966.

———. *Rhetorics*. Edited by W. D. Ross. Oxford: Clarendon, 1959.

Augustine. *Confessions*. Translated by Henry Chadwick. Oxford: Oxford University Press, 1991.

———. *Homilies on the First Epistle of John*. Translated by Boniface Ramsey. New York: New City, 2008.

———. *On Music Book IV*. Translated by Martin Jacobsson. Stockholm: Almquist & Wiksell, 2002.

Baldwin of Canterbury. *Tractatus Septimus: De Salutatione Angelica, de triplici gratia dei*. Patrologia Latina 204. Alexandria, VA: Chadwyck-Healey, 1996.

Balthasar, Hans Urs von. *Epilogue*. Translated by Edward T. Oakes. San Francisco: Ignatius, 1987.

———. *The Glory of the Lord*. Vol. 1, *Seeing the Form*. Translated by Erasmo Leiva-Merikakis. Edited by John Riches. San Francisco: Ignatius, 1988.

———. *The Glory of the Lord*. Vol. 4, *The Realm of Metaphysics in Antiquity*. Translated by Brian McNeil et al. Edited by John Riches. San Francisco: Ignatius, 1989.

Baumgarten, A. G. *Aesthetica*. 1750. Reprint, Hildesheim: G. Olms, 1970.

Bede the Venerable. *The Ecclesial History of the English Nation*. Translated by L. C. Jane. New York: Cosimo, 2007.

Bernard of Clairvaux. *Sermones in Cantica Canticorum*. Patrologia Latina Database, vol. 183. Alexandria, VA: Chadwyck-Healey Inc., *1996*.

Bonaventure, St. *Collationes in Hexameron*. Edited by R. P. Delorme. Quaracchi, 1934. Available in English as *The Collations in Six Days*. Translated by Jose De Vinck. St. Bonaventure, NY: Franciscan, 1978.

———. *The Journey of the Soul into God* (*Itinerarium mentis ad deum*). Translated by Zachary Hayes. St. Bonaventure, NY: Franciscan, 2002.

———. *The Life of Saint Francis of Assisi*. Edited with a foreword by Edward Cardinal Manning. London: Tan, 2010.

Briggs, C. A., F. Brown, and S. R. Driver, eds. *A Hebrew and English Lexicon of the Old Testament*. Oxford: Clarendon, 1907.

Cassiodorus. *On the Liberal Arts*. Patrologia Latina 70. Alexandria, VA: Chadwyck-Healey, 1996.

De Bruyne, Edgar. *Etudes d'esthétique médiévale, en trios tomes*. Bruges: Éditions De Tempel, 1946 and Paris: Éditions Albin Michels, 1998.

Dionysius the Areopagite. *The Works of Dionysius the Areopagite*. 2 vols. Translated by John Parker. London: James Parker, 1897–99.

Dostoevksy, Fyodor. *The Brothers Karamazov: A Novel in Four Parts with Epilogue*. Translated by Richard Pevear and Larissa Volokhonsky. New York: Farrar, Straus and Giroux, 2002.

———. *The Idiot*. Translated by Constance Garnett. New York: Random House, 2003.

———. *Notes from the Underground*. Translated by Richard Pevear and Larissa Volokhonsky. New York: Random House, 1993.

Dupré, Louis. *Religious Mystery and Rational Reflection*. Grand Rapids: Eerdmans, 1998.

Eagleton, Terry. *The Ideology of the Aesthetic*. Oxford: Blackwell, 1990.

Ehrman, Bart D. *Did Jesus Exist? The Historical Argument for Jesus of Nazareth.* New York: HarperCollins, 2012.

Eriugena, John Scotus. *Periphyseon: The Division of Nature.* Translated by I. P. Sheldon-Williams. Washington, DC: Dumbarton Oaks, 1987.

Fields, Harvey J. *A Torah Commentary for Our Times: Exodus and Leviticus.* New York: URJ Books and Music, 1990.

Forte, Bruno. *The Portal of Beauty: Toward a Theology of Aesthetics.* Translated by David Glenday and Paul McPartlan. Grand Rapids: Eerdmans, 2009.

García-Rivera, Alejandro. *The Community of the Beautiful: A Theological Aesthetic.* Collegeville, MN: Liturgical, 1999.

———. *The Garden of God: A Theological Cosmology.* Minneapolis: Fortress, 2008.

Gilby, Thomas. *Poetic Experience: An Introduction to Thomist Aesthetics.* New York: Sheed and Ward, 1934.

Grant, Edward. "The Condemnation of 1277, God's Absolute Power, and Physical Thought in the Late Middle Ages." *Viator* 10 (1977) 211–44.

Hegel, G. F. W. *Sämtliche Werke (Jubiläumsausgabe).* Edited by Hermann Glockner. Vol. 19. Stuttgart: F. Frommann, 1930.

John Paul II, Paul. *Letter to Artists.* Chicago: Liturgy Training Publications, 1999.

Jones, Malcolm V. "Dostoevskii and Religion." In *A Cambridge Companion to Dostoevskii,* edited by W. J. Leatherbarrow, 148–74. Cambridge: Cambridge University Press, 2002.

Kant, Immanuel. *Critique of Judgment.* Translated by Werner S. Pluhar. Indianapolis: Hackett, 1987.

Kierkegaard, Søren. *Concluding Unscientific Postscript to Philosophical Fragments.* Edited and translated by Howard V. Hong and Edna H. Hong. Princeton: Princeton University Press, 1992.

———. *Either/Or.* Edited and translated by Howard V. Hong and Edna H. Hong. 2 vols. Princeton: Princeton University Press, 1987.

———. *Fear and Trembling and Repetition.* Edited and Translated by Howard V. Hong and Edna H. Hong. Princeton: Princeton University Press, 1983.

Lubac, Henri de. *The Mystery of the Supernatural.* Translated by Rosemary Sheed. New York: Crossroad, 1998.

———. *The Splendor of the Church.* Translated by Michael Mason. San Francisco: Ignatius, 1999.

Bibliography

Matera, Frank J. *God's Saving Grace: A Pauline Theology*. Grand Rapids: Eerdmans, 2012.

Mykytiuk, Lawrence. "Did Jesus Exist? Searching for Evidence Beyond the Bible." *Biblical Archaeology Review* 41 (2015) 41–76.

Moran, Dermot. *The Philosophy of John Scotus Eriugena: A Study of Idealism in the Middle Ages*. Cambridge: Cambridge University Press, 1989.

Pecknold, C. C. *Christianity and Politics: A Brief Guide to the History*. Eugene, OR: Cascade, 2010.

Pieper, Josef. *"Divine Madness": Plato's Case against Secular Humanism*. Translated by Lothar Krauth. San Francisco: Ignatius, 1955.

Plato. *The Phaedrus*. Translated by R. Hackforth. In *The Collected Dialogues, Including the Letters*, edited by Edith Hamilton and Huntington Cairns, 475–525. Princeton: Princeton University Press, 1961.

Plotinus. *The Enneads*. Translated by Stephen MacKenna and B. S. Page. Whitefish, MT: Kessinger, 2004.

Proclus. *On the Theology of Plato*. Translated by Thomas Taylor. London: Emerson's Library Press, 1820.

Przywara, Erich. *Analogia Entis: Metaphysics; Original Structure and Universal Rhythm*. Translated by John R. Betz and David Bentley Hart. Grand Rapids: Eerdmans, 2014.

Sokolowski, Robert. *The God of Faith and Reason*. Notre Dame: University of Notre Dame Press, 1982.

Tatarkiewicz, Wladyslaw. *History of Aesthetics, in Three Volumes*. Edited by Cyril Barrett. Translated by Adam and Ann Czerniawski. 3rd ed. London: Continuum, 1999.

Thomas of Cîteaux. *Commentarii in Cantica Canticorum*. Patrologia Latina Database, vol. 206. Alexandria, VA: Chadwyck-Healey Inc., *1996*.

Torrell, Jean-Pierre. *Saint Thomas Aquinas*. Translated by Robert Royal. 2 vols. Washington, DC: Catholic University of America Press, 1993.

Walsh, Sylvia. *Living Poetically: Kierkegaard's Existential Aesthetics*. University Park: Pennsylvania State University Press, 1996.

Weisheipl, James A. *Friar Thomas D'Aquino: His Life, Thought, and Works*. New York: Doubleday, 1974.

Williams, Rowan. *Dostoevsky: Faith, Language, and Fiction*. Waco: Baylor University Press, 2008.

Wright, N. T. *What Paul Really Said: Was Paul of Tarsus Really a Founder of Christianity?* Grand Rapids: Eerdmans, 1997.

CPSIA information can be obtained
at www.ICGtesting.com
Printed in the USA
LVHW02*1447150918
590259LV00012B/197/P